The Celebrity 411: Spotlight on Sharon Tate, Including her Personal Life, Famous Television Shows and Blockbusters such as The Beverly Hillbillies, Eye of the Devil, The Fearless Vampire Killers, Valley of the Dolls, her Career Debut, and More

Martha Martin

The role of the book within our culture is changing. The change is brought on by new ways to acquire & use content, the rapid dissemination of information and real-time peer collaboration on a global scale. Despite these changes one thing is clear--"the book" in it's traditional form continues to play an important role in learning and communication. The book you are holding in your hands utilizes the unique characteristics of the Internet -- relying on web infrastructure and collaborative tools to share and use resources in keeping with the characteristics of the medium (user-created, defying control, etc.)--while maintaining all the convenience and utility of a real book.

Contents

Articles

A Look at Sharon Tate — 1
- Sharon Tate — 1

Personal Life — 16
- Roman Polanski — 16
- Philippe Forquet — 32
- Doris Tate — 33

Professional Career – Filmography — 36
- Barabbas (1961 film) — 36
- Hemingway's Adventures of a Young Man — 39
- The Americanization of Emily — 41
- Eye of the Devil — 45
- Don't Make Waves — 47
- The Fearless Vampire Killers — 50
- Valley of the Dolls (film) — 54
- Rosemary's Baby (film) — 60
- The Wrecking Crew (1969 film) — 67
- The Thirteen Chairs — 71

Famous Co-stars — 75
- Julie Andrews — 75
- Tony Curtis — 89

TV Appearances — 97
- Mister Ed — 97

The Beverly Hillbillies	105
The Man from U.N.C.L.E.	122

Death — **142**

Victim impact statement	142

References

Article Sources and Contributors	145
Image Sources, Licenses and Contributors	146

A Look at Sharon Tate

Sharon Tate

Sharon Tate	
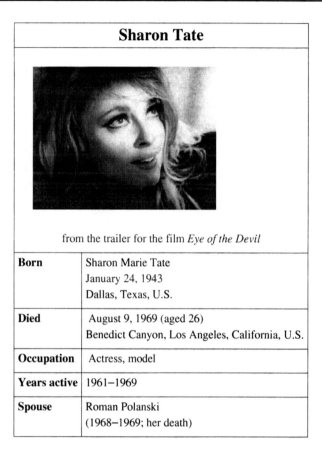 from the trailer for the film *Eye of the Devil*	
Born	Sharon Marie Tate January 24, 1943 Dallas, Texas, U.S.
Died	August 9, 1969 (aged 26) Benedict Canyon, Los Angeles, California, U.S.
Occupation	Actress, model
Years active	1961–1969
Spouse	Roman Polanski (1968–1969; her death)

Sharon Marie Tate (January 24, 1943 – August 9, 1969) was an American actress. During the 1960s she played small television roles before appearing in several films. After receiving positive reviews for her comedic performances, she was hailed as one of Hollywood's promising newcomers and was nominated for a Golden Globe Award for her performance in *Valley of the Dolls* (1967). She also appeared regularly in fashion magazines as a model and cover girl.

Married to the film director Roman Polanski in 1968, Tate was eight and a half months pregnant when she was murdered in her home, along with four others, by followers of Charles Manson.

A decade after the murders, Tate's mother, Doris, in response to the growing cult status of the killers and the possibility that any of them might be granted parole, organized a public campaign against what she considered shortcomings in the state's corrections system which led to amendments to the California criminal law in 1982, which allowed crime victims and their families to make victim impact statements during sentencing and at parole hearings. Doris Tate was the first person to make such an impact statement under the new law, when she spoke at the parole hearing of one of her daughter's killers, Charles "Tex" Watson. She later said that she believed the changes in the law had afforded her daughter dignity that had been denied her before, and that she had been able to "help transform Sharon's legacy from murder victim to a symbol of victims' rights".

Life and career

Childhood and early acting career

Sharon Tate was born in Dallas, Texas, the first of three daughters, to Paul Tate, a United States Army officer, and his wife, Doris. At six months of age, Sharon Tate won the "Miss Tiny Tot of Dallas Pageant", but the Tates held no show business ambitions for their daughter. Paul Tate was promoted and transferred several times. By age 16, Sharon Tate had lived in six different American cities, and she found it difficult to maintain friendships. Her family described her as shy and lacking in self-confidence, and as an adult Sharon Tate commented that people often misinterpreted her shyness for aloofness until they knew her better.

As she matured, people commented on her beauty; she began entering beauty pageants, winning the title of "Miss Richland" in 1959. She spoke of her ambition to study psychiatry, and also stated her intention to compete in the "Miss Washington" pageant in 1960, but before she could follow either course of action, Paul Tate was transferred to Italy, taking his family with him.

On arriving in Verona, Sharon Tate learned that she had become a local celebrity owing to the publication of a photograph of her in a bathing suit on the cover of the military newspaper *Stars and Stripes*. She discovered a kinship with other students at the American school she attended in nearby Vicenza, recognizing that their backgrounds and feelings of separation were similar to her own, and for the first time in her life began to form lasting friendships. Tate and her friends became interested in the filming of *Adventures of a Young Man*, which was being made nearby with Paul Newman, Susan Strasberg and Richard Beymer, and obtained parts as film extras. Beymer noticed Tate in the crowd and introduced himself, and the two dated during the production of the film, with Beymer encouraging Tate to pursue a film career. In 1961, Tate was employed by the singer Pat Boone, and appeared with him in a television special he made in Venice.

Tate (at right wearing a dark wig) as Janet Trego in the 1964 "Giant Jackrabbitt" episode of *The Beverly Hillbillies* with Max Baer, Jr. and Nancy Kulp

Later that year, when *Barabbas* was being filmed near Verona, Tate was once again hired as an extra. Actor Jack Palance was impressed by her appearance and her attitude, although her role was too small to judge her talent. He arranged a screen test for her in Rome, but this did not lead to further work. Tate returned to the United States alone, saying she wanted to further her studies, but tried to find film work. After a few months, Doris Tate, who feared for her daughter's safety, suffered a nervous breakdown and, after much coercion from her family, Tate returned to Italy.

The Tate family returned to the United States in 1962, and Sharon Tate moved to Los Angeles, where she contacted Richard Beymer's agent, Harold Gefsky. After their first meeting Gefsky agreed to represent her, and secured work for her in television and magazine advertisements. In 1963 he introduced her to Martin Ransohoff, director of Filmways, Inc., who signed her to a seven-year contract. Tate was considered for a lead role on *Petticoat Junction*, but Ransohoff realized that she was too inexperienced to handle an important role. He gave her small parts in *Mr. Ed* and *The Beverly Hillbillies* to help her gain experience. Ransohoff signed Tate to an exclusive seven year contract but kept her under wraps until he felt she was ready to appear in substantial film roles. "Mr. Ransohoff didn't want the audience to see me till I was ready," Tate was quoted in a 1967 article in *Playboy* magazine.

During this time Tate met the French actor Philippe Forquet, and began a relationship with him. They became engaged, but the relationship was volatile and they frequently quarreled. After a violent confrontation with Forquet, Tate required hospital treatment for her injuries, and subsequently ended the relationship.

In 1964, she met Jay Sebring, a former sailor who had established himself as a leading hair stylist in Hollywood. Tate later said that Sebring's nature was especially gentle, but when he proposed marriage she would not accept. She said that she would retire from acting as soon as she married, and at that time she intended to focus on her career.

Film career

In 1964, Tate made a screen test for Sam Peckinpah opposite Steve McQueen for the film *The Cincinnati Kid*. Ransohoff and Peckinpah agreed that Tate's timidity and lack of experience would cause her to flounder in such a large part, and she was rejected in favor of Tuesday Weld. She continued to gain experience with minor television appearances, and after she auditioned unsuccessfully for the role of Liesl in the film version of *The Sound of Music*, Ransohoff gave Tate walk-on roles in two motion pictures in which he was producer: *The Americanization of Emily* and *The Sandpiper*. In late 1965, Ransohoff finally gave Tate her first major role in a motion picture in the film, *Eye of the Devil*, co-starring David Niven, Deborah Kerr, Donald Pleasence, and David Hemmings. Tate and Sebring traveled to London to prepare for filming, where she met the Alexandrian Wiccan High Priest and High Priestess Alex and Maxine Sanders, the former of whom duly initiated her into Wicca. Meanwhile, as part of Ransohoff's promotion of Tate, he arranged the production of a short documentary called *All Eyes on Sharon Tate*, to be released at the same time as *Eye of the Devil*. It included an interview with *Eye of the Devil* director J. Lee Thompson, who expressed his initial doubts about Tate's potential with the comment "We even agreed that if after the first two weeks Sharon was not quite making it, that we would put her back in cold storage", but added that he soon realized Tate was "tremendously exciting".

Tate played Odile, a witch who exerts a mysterious power over a landowner, played by Niven, and his wife, played by Kerr. Although she did not have as many lines as the other actors, Tate's performance was considered crucial to the film, and she was required, more than the other cast members, to set an ethereal tone. Niven described her as a "great discovery", and Kerr said that with "a reasonable amount of luck", Tate would be a great success. In interviews, Tate commented on her good fortune in working with such professionals in her first film, and said that she had learned a lot about acting simply by watching Kerr at work. Much of the filming took place in France, and Sebring returned to Los Angeles to fulfill his business obligations. After filming Tate remained in London where she immersed herself in the fashion world and nightclubs. Around this time she met Roman Polanski.

Tate and Polanski later agreed that neither of them had been impressed by the other when they first met. Polanski was planning *The Fearless Vampire Killers*, which was being co-produced by Ransohoff, and had decided that he wanted the red-headed actress Jill St. John for the female lead. Ransohoff insisted that Polanski cast Tate, and after meeting with her, he agreed that she would be suitable on the condition that she wore a red wig during filming. The company traveled to Italy for filming where Tate's fluent Italian proved useful in communicating with the local crew members. A perfectionist, Polanski had little patience with the inexperienced Tate, and said in an interview that one scene had required seventy takes before he was satisfied. In addition to directing, Polanski also played one of the main characters, a guileless young man who is intrigued by Tate's character and begins a romance with her. As filming progressed, Polanski praised her performances and her confidence grew. They began a relationship, and Tate moved into Polanski's London apartment after filming ended. Jay Sebring traveled to London where he insisted on meeting Polanski. Although friends later said he was devastated, he befriended Polanski and remained Tate's closest confidante. Polanski later commented that Sebring was a lonely and isolated person, who viewed Tate and himself as his family.

Tate returned to the United States to film *Don't Make Waves* with Tony Curtis, leaving Polanski in London. Tate played the part of Malibu, and was allegedly the inspiration for the popular "Malibu Barbie" doll.[*citation needed*] The film was intended to capitalize on the popularity of beach movies and the music of such artists as the Beach Boys and Jan and Dean. Tate's character, billed by Metro-Goldwyn-Mayer publicity as "Malibu, Queen of the Surf", wore little more than a bikini for most of the film. Disappointed with the film, she began referring to herself sarcastically as "sexy little me". Before the film's release, a major publicity campaign resulted in photographs and life-sized cardboard figures of Sharon Tate being displayed in cinema foyers throughout the United States; a concurrent advertising campaign by *Coppertone* featured Tate. The film opened to poor reviews and mediocre ticket sales and Tate was quoted as confiding to a reporter, "It's a terrible movie", before adding, "Sometimes I say things I shouldn't. I guess I'm too outspoken."

Polanski returned to the United States, and was contracted by the head of Paramount Pictures, Robert Evans, to direct and write the screenplay for *Rosemary's Baby*, which was based on Ira Levin's novel of the same name. Polanski later admitted that he had wanted Tate to star in the film and had hoped that someone would suggest her, as he felt it inappropriate to make the suggestion himself. The producers did not suggest Tate, and Mia Farrow was cast. Tate reportedly provided ideas for some of the key scenes, including the scene in which the protagonist, Rosemary, is impregnated.[*citation needed*] She also appeared uncredited as a guest in a party scene. A frequent visitor to the set, she was photographed there by *Esquire* magazine and the resulting photographs generated considerable publicity for both Tate and the film.

A March 1967 article about Tate in *Playboy* magazine began, "This is the year that Sharon Tate happens..." and included six nude or partially nude photographs taken by Roman Polanski during filming of *The Fearless Vampire Killers*. Tate was optimistic: *Eye of the Devil* and *The Fearless Vampire Killers* were each due for release, and she had been signed to play a major role in the film version of *Valley of the Dolls*. One of the all-time bestsellers, the film version was highly publicized and anticipated, and while Tate acknowledged that such a prominent role should further her career, she confided to Polanski that she did not like either the book or the script.

Patty Duke, Barbara Parkins and Judy Garland were cast as the other leads. Susan Hayward replaced Garland a few weeks later when Garland was dismissed. Director Mark Robson was highly critical of the three principal actresses but, according to Duke, directed most of his criticism at Tate. Duke later said Robson "continually treated [Tate] like an imbecile, which she definitely was not, and she was very attuned and sensitive to this treatment." Polanski later quoted Robson as saying to him, "That's a great girl you're living with. Few actresses have her kind of vulnerability. She's got a great future."

In interviews during production, Tate expressed an affinity for her character, Jennifer North, an aspiring actress admired only for her body. Some magazines commented that Tate was viewed similarly and *Look* magazine published an unfavorable article about the three lead actresses, describing Tate as "a hopelessly stupid and vain starlet". Tate, Duke and Parkins developed a close friendship which continued after the completion of the film. During the shooting of *Valley of the Dolls*, Tate confided to Parkins that she was "madly in love" with Polanski. "Yes, there's no doubt that Roman is the man in my life," Tate was quoted as saying in the New York *Sunday News*. Tate promoted the film enthusiastically. She frequently commented on her admiration for Lee Grant, with whom she had played several dramatic scenes. Tate was quoted as saying, "I learned a great deal about acting in [Valley of the Dolls], particularly in my scenes with Lee Grant...She knows what acting is all about and everything she does, from little mannerisms to delivering her lines, is pure professionalism."

A journalist asked Tate to comment on her nude scene, and she replied,

> I have no qualms about it at all. I don't see any difference between being stark naked or fully dressed—if it's part of the job and it's done with meaning and intention. I honestly don't understand the big fuss made over nudity and sex in films. It's silly. On TV, the children can watch people murdering each other, which is a very unnatural thing, but they can't watch two people in the very natural process of making love. Now, really, that doesn't make any sense, does it?

An edited version of *The Fearless Vampire Killers* was released, and Polanski expressed disgust at Ransohoff for "butchering" his film. *Newsweek* called it "a witless travesty", and it was not profitable. Tate's performance was largely ignored in reviews, and when she was mentioned, it was usually in relation to her nude scenes. *Eye of the Devil* was released shortly after, and Metro-Goldwyn-Mayer attempted to build interest in Tate with its press release describing her as "one of the screen's most exciting new personalities". The film failed to find an audience, and most reviews were indifferent, neither praising nor condemning it. The *New York Times* wrote that one of the few highlights was Tate's "chillingly beautiful but expressionless performance".

The *All Eyes on Sharon Tate* documentary was used to publicize the film. Its fourteen minutes consisted of a number of scenes depicting Tate filming *Eye of the Devil*, dancing in nightclubs and sightseeing around London, and also contained a brief interview with her. Asked about her acting ambitions she replied, "I don't fool myself. I can't see myself doing Shakespeare." She spoke of her hopes of finding a niche in comedy, and in other interviews she expressed her desire to become "a light comedienne in the Carole Lombard style". She discussed the type of contemporary actress she wanted to emulate and explained that there were two in particular that she was influenced by: Faye Dunaway and Catherine Deneuve. Of the latter, she said, "I'd like to be an American Catherine Deneuve. She plays beautiful, sensitive, deep parts with a little bit of intelligence behind them."

Later in the year, *Valley of the Dolls* opened to almost uniformly negative reviews. Bosley Crowther wrote in *The New York Times*, "all a fairly respectful admirer of movies can do is laugh at it and turn away". *Newsweek* said that the film "has no more sense of its own ludicrousness than a village idiot stumbling in manure", but a later article read: "Astoundingly photogenic, infinitely curvaceous, Sharon Tate is one of the most smashing young things to hit Hollywood in a long time." The three lead actresses were castigated in numerous publications, including *The Saturday Review*, which wrote, "Ten years ago... Parkins, Duke and Tate would more likely have been playing the hat check girls than movie-queens; they are totally lacking in style, authority or charm." *The Hollywood Reporter* provided some positive comments, such as, "Sharon Tate emerges as the film's most sympathetic character... William H. Daniels' photographic caress of her faultless face and enormous absorbent eyes is stunning." Roger Ebert of the *Chicago Sun-Times* praised Tate as "a wonder to behold", but after describing the dialogue in one scene as "the most offensive and appalling vulgarity ever thrown up by any civilization", concluded that, "I will be unable to take her any more seriously as a sex symbol than Raquel Welch."

Marriage to Roman Polanski

In late 1967, Tate and Polanski returned to London, and were frequent subjects of newspaper and magazine articles. Tate was depicted as being untraditional and modern, and was quoted as saying that couples should live together before marrying. They were married in Chelsea, London on January 20, 1968 with considerable publicity. Polanski was dressed in what the press described as "Edwardian finery," while Tate was attired in a white minidress. The couple moved into Polanski's mews house off Eaton Square in Belgravia. Photographer Peter Evans later described them as "the imperfect couple. They were the Douglas Fairbanks/Mary Pickford of our time... Cool, nomadic, talented and nicely shocking."

While Tate reportedly wanted a traditional marriage, Polanski remained somewhat promiscuous and described Tate's attitude to his infidelity as "Sharon's big hang-up". He reminded Tate that she had promised that she would not try to change him. Tate accepted Polanski's conditions, though she confided to friends that she hoped he would change. Peter Evans quoted Tate as saying, "We have a good arrangement. Roman lies to me and I pretend to believe him."

Polanski urged Tate to end her association with Martin Ransohoff, and Tate began to place less importance on her career, until Polanski told her that he wanted to be married to "a hippie, not a housewife". The couple returned to Los Angeles and quickly became part of a social group that included some of the most successful young people in the film industry, including Steve McQueen, Warren Beatty, Mia Farrow, Peter Sellers, Jacqueline Bisset, Leslie Caron, Joan Collins, Joanna Pettet, Laurence Harvey, Peter Fonda and Jane Fonda, older film stars like Henry Fonda, Kirk Douglas, Yul Brynner and Danny Kaye, musicians such as Jim Morrison and the Mamas & the Papas, and record producer Terry Melcher and his girlfriend Candice Bergen. Jay Sebring remained one of the couple's most frequent companions. Polanski's circle of friends included people he had known since his youth in Poland such as Wojciech Frykowski and Frykowski's girlfriend, coffee heiress Abigail Folger. The couple moved into the Chateau Marmont Hotel in West Hollywood for a few months until they arranged to lease Patty Duke's home on Summit Ridge Drive in Beverly Hills during the latter part of 1968. The Polanski house was often full of strangers, and Tate regarded the casual atmosphere as part of the "free spirit" of the times, saying that she did not mind who came into her home as her motto was "live and let live". Her close friend Leslie Caron later commented that the Polanskis were too trusting — "to the point of recklessness" — and that she had been alarmed by it.

In the summer of 1968, Tate began her next film, *The Wrecking Crew* (1969), a comedy in which she played Freya Carlson, an accident-prone spy, who was also a romantic interest for star Dean Martin, playing Matt Helm. She performed her own stunts and was taught martial arts by Bruce Lee. The film was successful and brought Tate strong reviews, with many reviewers praising her comedic performance. The *New York Times* critic Vincent Canby criticized the film but wrote, "The only nice thing is Sharon Tate, a tall, really great-looking girl". Martin commented that he intended to make another "Matt Helm" film, and that he wanted Tate to reprise her role.

Around this time Tate was feted as a promising newcomer. She was nominated for a Golden Globe Award as "New Star of the Year – Actress" for her *Valley of the Dolls* performance.

She placed fourth behind Mia Farrow, Judy Geeson and Katharine Houghton for a "Golden Laurel" award as the year's "Most Promising Newcomer" with the results published in the *Motion Picture Exhibitor* magazine. She was also runner-up to Lynn Redgrave in the *Motion Picture Herald*'s poll for "The Star of Tomorrow", in which box-office drawing power was the main criterion for inclusion on the list. These results indicated that her career was beginning to accelerate and for her next film, Tate negotiated a fee of $150,000.

Tate became pregnant near the end of 1968, and on February 15, 1969 she and Polanski moved to 10050 Cielo Drive in Benedict Canyon. The house had previously been occupied by their friends, Terry Melcher and Candice Bergen. Tate and Polanski had visited it several times, and Tate was thrilled to learn it was available, referring to it as her "love house". At their new home, the Polanskis continued to be popular hosts for their large group of friends, although some of their friends still worried about the strange types who continued to show up at their parties. Encouraged by positive reviews of her comedic performances, Tate chose the comedy *The Thirteen Chairs* as her next project, as she later explained, largely for the opportunity to co-star with Orson Welles. In March 1969, she traveled to Italy to begin filming, while Polanski went to London to work on *The Day of the Dolphin*. Frykowski and Folger moved into the Cielo Drive house.

After completing *The Thirteen Chairs*, Tate joined Polanski in London. She posed in their apartment for photographer Terry O'Neill in casual domestic scenes such as opening baby gifts, and also completed a series of glamour photographs for the British magazine *Queen*. A journalist asked Tate in a late July interview if she believed in fate, to which she replied, "Certainly. My whole life has been decided by fate. I think something more powerful than we are decides our fates for us. I know one thing — I've never planned anything that ever happened to me."

She returned from London to Los Angeles, on July 20, 1969, traveling alone on the RMS *Queen Elizabeth*. Polanski was due to return on August 12 in time for the birth, and he asked Frykowski and Folger to stay in the house with Tate until then.

Death and aftermath

Murder

On August 8, 1969, Tate was two weeks from giving birth. She entertained two friends, actresses Joanna Pettet and Barbara Lewis, for lunch at her home, confiding in them her disappointment at Polanski's delay in returning from London. In the afternoon Polanski phoned her. Her younger sister Debra also called to ask if she and their sister Patti could spend the night with her, but Sharon declined. In the evening she went to her favorite restaurant, El Coyote, with Sebring, Frykowski and Folger, returning about 10:30 p.m.

During the night they were murdered by members of Charles Manson's "Family" and their bodies discovered the following morning by Tate's housekeeper, Winifred Chapman. Police arrived at the scene to find the body of a young man, later identified as Steven Parent, shot to death in his car, which was in the driveway. Inside the house, the bodies of Tate and Sebring were found in the living room; a long rope tied around each of their necks connected them. On the front lawn lay the bodies of Frykowski and Folger. All of the victims, except Parent, had been stabbed numerous times. The coroner's report for Tate noted that she had been stabbed sixteen times, and that "five of the wounds were in and of themselves fatal".

Police took the only survivor at the address, the caretaker William Garretson, for questioning. Garretson lived in the guest house which was located on the property, but a short distance from the house, and not immediately visible. As the first suspect, he was questioned and submitted to a polygraph test. He said that Parent had visited him at approximately 11:30 p.m. and left after a few minutes. Garretson said he had no involvement in the murders and did not know anything that could help the investigation. Police accepted his explanation and he was allowed to leave.

Polanski was informed of the murders and returned to Los Angeles where police, unable to determine a motive, questioned him about his wife and friends. On Wednesday, August 13, Tate was interred in the Holy Cross Cemetery, Culver City, California, with her son, Paul Richard Polanski (named posthumously for Polanski's and Tate's fathers), in her arms. Sebring's funeral took place later the same day; the funerals were scheduled several hours apart to allow mutual friends to attend both.

Life magazine devoted a lengthy article to the murders and featured photographs of the crime scenes. Polanski was interviewed for the article and allowed himself to be photographed in the living room where Tate and Sebring had died, Tate's dried blood clearly visible on the floor in front of him. Widely criticized for his actions, he argued that he wanted to know who was responsible and was willing to shock the magazine's readers in the hope that someone would come forward with information.

Curiosity about the victims led to the re-release of Tate's films, achieving greater popularity than they had in their initial runs. Some newspapers began to speculate on the motives for the murders. Some of the published photographs of Tate were allegedly taken at a Satanic ritual, but were later proven to have been production photographs from *Eye of the Devil*. Friends spoke out against the portrayal of Tate by some elements of the media. Mia Farrow said she was as "sweet and pure a human being as I have ever known", while Patty Duke remembered her as "a gentle, gentle creature. I was crazy about her, and I don't know anyone who wasn't". Polanski berated a crowd of journalists at a press conference, saying that many times they had written that Tate "was beautiful. Maybe the most beautiful woman in the world. But did you ever write how good she was?". Peter Evans later quoted the actor Laurence Harvey, who commented on Polanski immediately after the murders, "This could destroy Roman. Marriage vows mean nothing to him but few men have adored a woman as much as he adored Sharon."

Polanski later admitted that in the months following the murders he suspected various friends and associates, and his paranoia subsided only when the killers were arrested. Newspapers claimed that many Hollywood stars were moving out of the city, while others were reported to have installed security systems in their homes. Writer Dominick Dunne later recalled the tension:

> The shock waves that went through the town were beyond anything I had ever seen before. People were convinced that the rich and famous of the community were in peril. Children were sent out of town. Guards were hired. Steve McQueen packed a gun when he went to Jay Sebring's funeral.

Arrest and trial of the Manson Family

In November 1969, while in prison in connection with a car theft, Susan Atkins boasted to an inmate that she was responsible for the murder of Sharon Tate. This led to her indictment, along with the accomplices she named, Charles Manson, Charles "Tex" Watson, Patricia Krenwinkel and Linda Kasabian. Atkins also revealed that the murders of Leno and Rosemary LaBianca in Los Feliz, Los Angeles, the night after the Tate murders, were also committed by "Family" members, and incriminated Leslie Van Houten as a participant in the second murder.

The Los Angeles County District Attorney offered Susan Atkins a deal that guaranteed they would not seek the death penalty against her for any of the current charges in exchange for her grand jury and trial testimony. Atkins testified before the grand jury that she had been unable to stab Sharon Tate and that she was killed by Watson, a contradiction of statements she had made prior to her arrest. Atkins refused to cooperate further, forcing the District Attorney's office to withdraw its offer. An offer of immunity against prosecution was made to Kasabian in exchange for her agreement to provide complete testimony at any trial, against any of the defendants. Assistant District Attorney Vincent Bugliosi wrote later that he believed Kasabian would be more acceptable to the jurors because she had not killed anyone. In his book *Will You Die For Me*, Charles Watson later confessed to the murder saying Atkins didn't even touch her.

On June 15, 1970, Manson, Atkins, Krenwinkel, and Van Houten were tried while Watson remained in Texas fighting extradition. The details of the trial were reported throughout the world. Kasabian was a reliable and consistent witness. She testified about a hippie group and its leader Charles Manson, a thwarted musician who believed that a race war was imminent. He believed that the music of The Beatles warned of the coming holocaust, which he referred to as *Helter Skelter*, after the Beatles song, and also believed that only the "chosen", his "family", would survive. Briefly associated with Terry Melcher, Manson had believed that Melcher would foster his musical aspirations; when this did not occur, Manson felt infuriated and betrayed. Manson believed that he would bring about the race war by having his followers slaughter wealthy people in their homes and cast suspicion on militant groups such as the Black Panthers. Manson expected these groups to win the race war, and predicted that they would make him their leader when they realized they were too inept to govern the new society. He had been to 10050 Cielo Drive, and although he knew that Melcher had moved, the house represented his rejection by the show business establishment. He instructed Watson, Atkins, Krenwinkel, and Kasabian to go to the house "and kill everyone there", while he remained in their camp at Spahn's Movie Ranch.

Kasabian's and Atkins' testimony provided details that had not previously been reported to the public. When the group scaled a fence surrounding the property, they were seen by Steven Parent, who was leaving in his car. Watson approached the vehicle and ordered it to stop. Parent asked Watson not to hurt him, and promised that he would not say anything, but Watson's response was to slash Parent with a knife and shoot him four times. Watson then instructed Kasabian to remain outside and keep watch while the others entered the house. The four occupants were rounded up into the living room and tied together at gunpoint. When Watson ordered the occupants to lie on their stomachs, Jay Sebring urged the intruders to consider Tate's pregnancy and not harm her. Watson immediately shot Sebring. Wojciech Frykowski and Abigail Folger escaped, running in different directions onto the front lawn, where they were each overtaken and killed. Tate remained in the house and begged for her child's life, pleading that the group abduct Tate and allow her to give birth before murdering her. Atkins testified that she had told Tate she would receive no mercy. Tate was stabbed sixteen times, and Atkins dipped a towel in Tate's blood to write "PIG" on the front door. They left Tate's house after midnight and returned to Spahn Ranch.

During the penalty phase of the trail, Atkins was again questioned about her attitude to Tate and her role in Tate's death. She said, "They didn't even look like people... I didn't relate to Sharon Tate as being anything but a store mannequin... [Tate] sounded just like an IBM machine... She kept begging and pleading and pleading and begging, and I got sick of listening to her, so I stabbed her." The defendants were found guilty and sentenced to death on March 29, 1971. Watson was tried separately after extradition from Texas. Psychiatrists testified that he appeared to be feigning insanity, and while he admitted his role in all of the killings, he refused to acknowledge his responsibility, and was widely quoted by the press when he stated that he had not noticed that Sharon Tate was pregnant. He was found guilty and sentenced to death on October 21, 1971. The death sentences were later automatically commuted to life in prison after the California Supreme Court's People v. Anderson decision resulted in the invalidation of all death sentences imposed in California before 1972. As of 2010, Manson, Watson, Krenwinkel, and Van Houten remain incarcerated. Atkins died in prison on September 24, 2009.

Legacy

In the early 1980s, Stephen Kay, who had worked for the prosecution in the trial, became alarmed that Leslie Van Houten had gathered 900 signatures on a petition for her parole. He contacted Sharon Tate's mother, who said she was sure she could do better, and the two mounted a publicity campaign, collecting over 350,000 signatures supporting the denial of parole. Van Houten had been seen as the most likely of the killers to be paroled; following Kay's and Tate's efforts, her petition was denied. Doris Tate became a vocal advocate for victims' rights and, in discussing her daughter's murder and meeting other crime victims, assumed the role of counselor, using her profile to encourage public discussion and criticism of the corrections system.

For the rest of her life she strongly campaigned against the parole of each of the Manson killers, and worked closely with other victims of violent crime. Several times she confronted Charles Watson at parole hearings, explaining, "I feel that Sharon has to be represented in that hearing room. If they're [the killers] pleading for their lives, then I have to be there representing her." She addressed Watson directly during her victim impact statement in 1984: "What mercy, sir, did you show my daughter when she was begging for her life? What mercy did you show my daughter when she said, 'Give me two weeks to have my baby and then you can kill me'?.... When will Sharon come up for parole? Will these seven victims and possibly more walk out of their graves if you get paroled? You cannot be trusted."

In 1992, President George H. W. Bush recognized Doris Tate as one of his "thousand points of light" for her volunteer work on behalf of victims' rights. By this time Tate had been diagnosed with a malignant brain tumor and her health and strength were failing; her meeting with Bush marked her final public appearance. When she died later that year, her youngest daughter Patti continued her work. She contributed to the 1993 foundation of the **Doris Tate Crime Victims Bureau**, a non-profit organization which aims to influence crime legislation throughout the United States and to give greater rights and protection to victims of violent crime. In 1995, the "Doris Tate Crime Victims Foundation" was founded as a non-profit organization to promote public awareness of the judicial system and to provide support to the victims of violent crime.

Patti Tate confronted David Geffen and board members of Geffen Records in 1993 over plans to include a song written by Charles Manson on the Guns N' Roses album *"The Spaghetti Incident?"*. She commented to a journalist that the record company was "putting Manson up on a pedestal for young people who don't know who he is to worship like an idol."

After Patti's death from breast cancer in 2000, her older sister Debra continued to represent the Tate family at parole hearings. Debra Tate said of the killers: "They don't show any personal responsibility. They haven't made atonement to any one of my family members." She has also unsuccessfully lobbied for Sharon Tate to be awarded a star on the Hollywood Walk of Fame.

Colonel Paul Tate preferred not to make public comments; however, he was a constant presence during the murder trial, and in the following years attended parole hearings with his wife, and wrote letters to authorities in which he strongly opposed any suggestion of parole. He died in May 2005.

Roman Polanski gave away all of his possessions after the murders, unable to bear any reminders of the period that he called "the happiest I ever was in my life". He remained in Los Angeles until the killers were arrested and then traveled to Europe. His 1979 film *Tess* was dedicated "For Sharon", as Tate had read Thomas Hardy's *Tess of the d'Urbervilles* during her final stay with Polanski in London, and had left it for him to read with the comment that it would be a good story for them to film together. He tried to explain his anguish after the murder of his wife and unborn son in his 1984 autobiography *Roman by Polanski*, saying "Since Sharon's death, and despite appearances to the contrary, my enjoyment of life has been incomplete. In moments of unbearable personal tragedy some people find solace in religion. In my case the opposite happened. Any religious faith I had was shattered by Sharon's murder. It reinforced my faith in the absurd."

In July 2005 Polanski successfully sued *Vanity Fair* magazine for libel after it stated that he had tried to seduce a woman on his way to Tate's funeral. Among the witnesses who testified on his behalf were Debra Tate and Mia Farrow. Describing Polanski immediately after Tate's death, Farrow testified, "Of this I can be sure — of his frame of mind when we were there, of what we talked about, of his utter sense of loss, of despair and bewilderment and shock and love — a love that he had lost." At the conclusion of the case, Polanski read a statement, saying in part, "The memory of my late wife Sharon Tate was at the forefront of my mind in bringing this action."

The murders committed by the Manson "Family" have been described by social commentators as one of the defining moments of the 1960s. Joan Didion wrote, "Many people I know in Los Angeles believe that the Sixties ended abruptly on August 9, 1969, ended at the exact moment when word of the murders on Cielo Drive traveled like brushfire through the community, and in a sense this is true. The tension broke that day. The paranoia was fulfilled."

Sharon Tate's work as an actress has been reassessed after her death, with contemporary film writers and critics such as Leonard Maltin describing her potential as a comedienne. A restored version of *The Fearless Vampire Killers* more closely resembles Polanski's intention. Maltin lauded the film as "near-brilliant" and Tate's work in *Don't Make Waves* and *The Wrecking Crew* as her two best performances, as well as the best indicators of the career she might have established. *Eye of the Devil* with its supernatural themes, and *Valley of the Dolls*, with its overstated melodrama, have each achieved a degree of cult status.

Tate's biographer, Greg King, holds a view often expressed by members of the Tate family, writing in *Sharon Tate and the Manson Murders* (2000): "Sharon's real legacy lies not in her movies or in her television work. The very fact that, today, victims or their families in California are able to sit before those convicted of a crime and have a voice in the sentencing at trials or at parole hearings, is largely due to the work of Doris [and Patti] Tate. Their years of devotion to Sharon's memory and dedication to victims' rights... have helped transform Sharon from mere victim, [and] restore a human face to one of the twentieth century's most infamous crimes."

Filmography

Year	Film	Role	Notes
1961	*Barabbas*	Patrician in Arena	uncredited
1962	*Hemingway's Adventures of a Young Man*	undetermined role	uncredited
1963–1965	*The Beverly Hillbillies*	Janet Trego	15 episodes
1963	*Mister Ed*	Telephone Operator Sailor's Girl	Episode "Love Thy New Neighbor" Episode "Ed Discovers America"
1964	*The Americanization of Emily*	Beautiful Girl	uncredited
1965	*The Man from U.N.C.L.E.*	Therapist	Episode "The Girls of Nazarone Affair"
1966	*Eye of the Devil*	Odile de Caray	
1967	*The Fearless Vampire Killers*	Sarah Shagal	
1967	*Don't Make Waves*	Malibu	
1967	*Valley of the Dolls*	Jennifer North	
1968	*Rosemary's Baby*	Girl at Party	uncredited
1968	*The Wrecking Crew*	Freya Carlson	
1969	*The Thirteen Chairs* (also known as *12+1*)	Pat	released posthumously

References

External links

Informational sites

- Official website [1]
- Sharon Tate Official Fanlisting [2]
- Sharon Tate [3] at the Internet Movie Database
- Sharon Tate [4] at Find a Grave
- SharonTate.Info [5]

Crime sites

- CharlieManson.com – Extensive information on the Manson Family [6]
- CieloDrive.com – The Story of the Manson Family and Their Victims [7]
- The Crime Library [8]

Personal Life

Roman Polanski

Roman Polanski	
Polanski with a Crystal Globe, 2005	
Born	Raymond (Rajmund) Polański 18 August 1933 Paris, France
Occupation	Actor, director, producer, screenwriter
Years active	1953–present
Spouse	Barbara Lass (1959–1962) Sharon Tate (1968–1969) Emmanuelle Seigner (1989–present)

Roman Polanski (Polish: *Roman Polański*, Polish pronunciation: [ˈrɔman pɔˈlaɲskʲi]; born 18 August 1933) is a Polish-French film director, producer, writer and actor. Born in Paris to Polish parents, Polanski relocated with his family to Poland in 1937. After surviving the Holocaust, he continued his education in Poland and became a critically acclaimed director of both art house and commercial films. Polanski's first feature-length film, *Knife in the Water* (1962), made in Poland, was nominated for an Academy Award for Best Foreign Language Film. He has since received five more Oscar nominations, and in 2002 received the Academy Award for Best Director for his film, *The Pianist*. He has also been the recipient of two Baftas, four Césars, a Golden Globe and the Palme d'Or. He left Poland in 1961 to live in France for several years, then moved to the United Kingdom where he collaborated with Gérard Brach on three films, beginning with *Repulsion* (1965). In 1968 he moved to the United States, immediately cementing his burgeoning directing status with the 1968 groundbreaking Academy Award winning horror film *Rosemary's Baby*.

In 1969, Polanski's pregnant wife, Sharon Tate, was murdered while staying at the Polanski's Benedict Canyon home above Los Angeles by members of the Manson Family. Following Tate's death, Polanski returned to Europe and spent much of his time in Paris and Gstaad, but did not make another film until he filmed *Macbeth* (1971) in England. The following year he went to Italy to make *What?* (1973) and subsequently spent the next five years living near Rome. However, he traveled to Hollywood to direct *Chinatown* (1974) for Paramount Pictures, with Robert Evans serving as producer. The film was nominated for eleven Academy Awards, and was a critical and box-office success; the script by Robert Towne won for Best Original Screenplay. Polanski's next film, *The Tenant* (1976), was shot in France, and completed the "Apartment Trilogy", following *Repulsion* and *Rosemary's Baby*.

In 1977, after a photo shoot in Los Angeles, Polanski was arrested for the sexual abuse of a 13 year old girl. He was charged with rape but pleaded guilty to unlawful sex with a minor. To avoid sentencing, Polanski fled to his home in London, and then moved on to France the following day. He has had a U.S. arrest warrant outstanding since then, and an international arrest warrant since 2005.

Polanski continued to make films such as *The Pianist* (2002), a World War II-set adaptation of Jewish-Polish musician Władysław Szpilman's autobiography of the same name, which echoed some of Polanski's earlier life experiences. Like Szpilman, Polanski escaped the ghetto and the concentration camps while family members were killed. The film won three Academy Awards including Best Director, the Cannes Film Festival's Palme d'Or, and seven French César Awards including Best Picture and Best Director. He then released the successful films *Oliver Twist* (2005), *To Each His Own Cinema* (2007), and *The Ghost Writer* (2010), completed while under house arrest.

In September 2009, Polanski was arrested by Swiss police, at the request of U.S. authorities, when he traveled to receive a lifetime achievement award at the Zurich Film Festival. In October 2009, the U.S. requested his extradition; however, on July 12, 2010, the Swiss rejected that request and instead declared him a "free man" after releasing him from custody.

Early life

Polanski was born as Rajmund Roman Thierry Polański in Paris, France, the son of Bula (*née* Katz-Przedborska) and Ryszard Polański (né Liebling), a painter and plastics manufacturer. His mother had a daughter, Annette, by her previous husband. Annette managed to survive Auschwitz, where her mother died, and left Poland forever for France. His father was Jewish and his Russian-born mother had been raised Roman Catholic. His mother's father was Jewish, but not observant.[citation needed] Ryszard Liebling had changed his surname to Polański in early 1932. The Polański family moved back to the Polish city of Kraków in 1936, and were living there when the World War II began with the invasion of Poland. Neither of Roman Polanski's parents was religious. Kraków was soon occupied by the German forces. Nazi racial and religious purity laws made the Polańskis targets of persecution and forced them into the Kraków Ghetto, along with thousands of the city's Jews.

His father survived the Mauthausen-Gusen concentration camp in Austria, but his mother perished at Auschwitz. Polański himself escaped the Kraków Ghetto in 1943 and survived the war using the name Romek Wilk with the help of some Polish Roman Catholic families. As a Jewish child in hiding, he behaved outwardly as a Roman Catholic, although he was never baptized as such. After the war he was reunited with his father and moved back to Kraków. Roman Polanski's father married Wanda Zajączkowska, but Roman disliked his stepmother, which further estranged father and son, who had never been able to establish an intimate relationship. Ryszard Polański died of cancer in 1984.

Career

Polanski attended the National Film School in Łódź, the third-largest city in Poland. In the 1950s Polanski took up acting, appearing in Andrzej Wajda's *Pokolenie* (*A Generation*, 1954) and in the same year in Silik Sternfeld's *Zaczarowany rower* (*Enchanted Bicycle* or *Magical Bicycle*). Polanski's directorial debut was also in 1955 with a short film *Rower* (*Bicycle*). *Rower* is a semi-autobiographical feature film, believed to be lost, which also starred Polanski. It refers to his real-life violent altercation with a notorious Kraków felon, Janusz Dziuba, who arranged to sell Polanski a bike, but instead beat him badly and stole his money. In real life the offender was arrested while fleeing after fracturing Polanski's skull, and executed for three murders, out of eight prior such assaults, which he had committed. Several other short films made during his study at Łódź gained him considerable recognition, particularly *Two Men and a Wardrobe* (1958) and *When Angels Fall* (1959). He graduated in 1959.

Polanski's star on the Łódź walk of fame

Polanski's first feature-length film, *Knife in the Water* (1962), was also the first significant Polish film after WWII that did not have a war theme. Scripted by Jerzy Skolimowski, Jakub Goldberg and Polanski, *Knife in the Water* is about a wealthy, unhappily married couple who decide to take a mysterious hitchhiker with them on a weekend boating excursion. A dark and unsettling work, Polanski's debut feature subtly evinces a profound pessimism about human relationships with regard to the psychological dynamics and moral consequences of status envy and sexual jealousy. *Knife in the Water* was a major commercial success in the West and gave Polanski an international reputation. The film also earned its director his first Academy Award nomination (Best Foreign Language Film, 1963).

Despite his reputation as a major Polish filmmaker, Polanski left then-communist Poland and moved to France, where he had already made two notable short films in 1961: *The Fat and the Lean* and *Mammals*. While in France, Polanski contributed one segment ("La rivière de diamants") to the French-produced omnibus film, *Les plus belles escroqueries du monde* (English title: *The Beautiful Swindlers*) in 1964. However, Polanski found that in the early 1960s the French film industry was generally unwilling to support a rising filmmaker whom they viewed as a cultural Pole and not a Frenchman.

Gérard Brach collaborations

Polanski made three feature films in England, based on original scripts written by himself and Gérard Brach, a frequent collaborator. *Repulsion* (1965) is a psychological horror film focusing on a young Belgian woman named Carol (Catherine Deneuve), who is living in London with her older sister (Yvonne Furneaux). While working as a beautician's assistant at a salon, Carol is often disturbed by the physical decrepitude of her elderly clients, and throughout the course of the film, she becomes increasingly distressed by sexual advances from the men around her. Her sister departs for a holiday in Italy with a boyfriend, and Carol is left alone in their shared apartment flat. Carol's disordered mind finally breaks from reality as actual threats of domestic and sexual invasion blend into grotesque paranoid hallucinations, causing her to respond with desperate, deadly acts of violence. The film's themes, situations, visual motifs, and effects clearly reflect the influence of early surrealist cinema as well as horror movies of the 1950s – particularly Luis Buñuel's *Un chien Andalou*, Jean Cocteau's *The Blood of a Poet*, Henri-Georges Clouzot's *Diabolique* and Alfred Hitchcock's *Psycho*.

Cul-de-Sac (1966) is a bleak nihilist tragicomedy filmed on location in Northumberland. The general tone and the basic premise of the film owes a great deal to Samuel Beckett's *Waiting for Godot*, along with aspects of Harold Pinter's *The Birthday Party*. Indeed, the original title for the film was *When Katelbach Comes* (named after the actor André Katelbach, who played the role of the master in Polanski's very Beckettian 1961 short film *The Fat and the Lean*), and among the cast was Jack MacGowran, a veteran of Beckett's stage and television work. The film's setup concerns two gangsters, Dickie and Albie (Lionel Stander and MacGowran), who are on the run after a heist went wrong. The film opens with Dickie pushing their broken-down car along the tidal causeway of Lindisfarne island. It is implied that the shootout which occurred during the heist had left Albie bleeding and paralyzed, and Dickie, who is also wounded but still mobile, now seeks to contact their underworld boss, Katelbach. (Like Beckett's Godot, Katelbach is frequently alluded to throughout the course of the film, but never actually appears.) As he searches the island, Dickie discovers that the famous medieval castle is inhabited by an effeminate and neurotically excitable middle-aged Englishman named George (Donald Pleasence), and his adulterous, nymphomaniacal young French wife, Teresa (Françoise Dorléac, Catherine Deneuve's older sister). A series of absurd mishaps, both farcical and tragic, ensues when Dickie decides to take the couple hostage in their castle as he waits (in vain) for further instructions from the mysterious Katelbach.

The Fearless Vampire Killers (1967) is a parody of vampire films (particularly those made by Hammer Studios) which was filmed using elaborate sets built on sound stages in London with additional location photography in the Alps (particularly Urtijëi, an Italian ski resort in the Dolomites). The plot concerns a buffoonish professor named Abronsius (Jack MacGowran) and his clumsy assistant, Alfred (played by Polanski himself), who are traveling through Transylvania in search of vampires. The two of them arrive in a small village near a vampire-infested castle, which they plan to examine. While taking lodgings at the village tavern, Alfred falls in love with Sarah, the local innkeeper's daughter (played by Polanski's future wife, Sharon Tate). Shortly after, Sarah is abducted by the vampires and taken to the castle. The rest of the film concerns Abronsius and Alfred's madcap efforts to penetrate the castle walls and rescue the girl. The ironic and macabre ending is classic Polanski. *The Fearless Vampire Killers* was Polanski's first feature to be photographed in color with the use of Panavision lenses (the aspect ratio is 2.35:1). The film's striking visual style, with its snow-covered, fairy-tale landscapes, recalls the work of Soviet fantasy filmmakers Aleksandr Ptushko and Alexander Row. Similarly, the richly textured, moonlit-winter-blue color schemes of the village and the snowy valleys evoke the magical, kaleidoscopic paintings of the great Russian-Jewish artist Marc Chagall, who provides the namesake for the innkeeper in the film. The film is also notable in that it features Polanski's love of winter sports, particularly skiing. In this respect *The Fearless Vampire Killers* recalls Polanski's 1961 short film *Mammals*.

Polanski and Tate began a relationship during filming, and were married in London on 20 January 1968.

Move to United States

In *Rosemary's Baby: A Retrospective*, a featurette on the DVD release of the film, Polanski, Paramount Pictures executive Robert Evans, and production designer Richard Sylbert reminisce at length about the production. Evans recalled William Castle brought him the galley proofs of the novel *Rosemary's Baby* by Ira Levin and asked him to purchase the film rights even before Random House released the publication. The studio head recognized the commercial potential of the project and agreed with the stipulation that Castle, who had a reputation for low-budget horror films, could produce but not direct the film adaptation. Evans admired Polanski's European films and hoped he could convince him to make his American debut with *Rosemary's Baby* (1968). He knew Polanski was a ski buff who was anxious to make a film with the sport as its basis, so he sent him the script for *Downhill Racer* with the galleys for *Rosemary*. Polanski read the book non-stop through the night and called Evans the following morning to tell him he thought it was the more interesting project, and would like the opportunity to write as well as direct it. His first Hollywood film established his reputation as a major commercial filmmaker and both the novel and movie became commercial successes. A horror-thriller set in the trendy Manhattan apartment building "The Dakota", the story is about Rosemary Woodhouse (Mia Farrow), an innocent young housewife, originally from Omaha, who is impregnated by the devil after her narcissistic and ambitious actor husband, Guy (John Cassavetes), offers her womb to a coven of local satanists in exchange for stardom. Much of the film concerns Rosemary's suspicions and her increasingly successful attempts to uncover the truth of what is going on. Polanski's screenplay adaptation earned him a second Academy Award nomination. In April 1969, Polanski's friend and collaborator, the composer Krzysztof Komeda, died from head injuries sustained from a skiing accident, though other accounts of the cause of his death exist. After the short *Two Men and a Wardrobe*, Komeda went on to compose the score to all of Polanski's feature films (with the exception of *Repulsion*).

After making his next two films in Europe, Polanski returned to Hollywood in 1973 to direct *Chinatown* for Paramount Pictures with Robert Evans serving as producer. The film was nominated for a total of 11 Academy Awards; stars Jack Nicholson and Faye Dunaway both received Oscar nominations for their roles, and the script by Robert Towne won for Best Original Screenplay. Polanski appears in a cameo role as a hoodlum who slices Nicholson's nose with a knife in a failed attempt to scare him off the case.

Return to Europe

On 9 August 1969, while Polanski was working in London, Sharon Tate and four other people were murdered at the Polanskis' residence in Los Angeles. Polanski abandoned his project and did not resume working until the production of Shakespeare's *The Tragedy of Macbeth* (1971). Jon Finch and Francesca Annis appeared in the lead roles. He adapted Shakespeare's original text into a screenplay with the British theater critic Kenneth Tynan, and gained financing for the project through his friendship with Victor Lownes, who was an executive for *Playboy* magazine in London at the time. Polanski wanted to make the film in the play's actual historical setting of Scotland, but while scouting for locations there he could find no suitable sites that were still unmarked by telephone poles and other such modern installations. He eventually chose to shoot in an area of Britain which would provide him with a much more convincing medieval landscape complete with picturesque Norman castles: the rugged environs of Snowdonia National Park in Gwynedd, North Wales. The production took six months to complete and exceeded its initial budget by at least $500,000 mostly because of weather problems (it rained frequently during the location filming in Wales) as well as Polanski's insistence on shooting multiple takes of several technically challenging scenes in these adverse conditions. When the film finally premiered in December 1971, a number of critics were disturbed by its rampant violence as well as the overwhelming nightmarish atmosphere and unredeemed nihilism of Polanski's very modernist interpretation of Shakespeare (influenced by the writings of Polish drama critic and theoretician, Jan Kott). The violent and bloody nature of the film drew comment; film critic Pauline Kael wrote that the "corpses and murders ... so dominate the material that it's difficult to pay attention to the poetry." Polanski was reported to have responded to a comment during filming that the blood-letting was unrealistic, with "You didn't see my house in California last summer. I know about bleeding." In his autobiography Polanski wrote that he wanted to be true to the violent nature of the work, and that he had been aware that his first project following Tate's murder, would be subject to scrutiny and probable cricitism regardless of the subject matter; if he had made a comedy he would have been perceived as callous.

Written by Polanski and previous collaborator Gérard Brach, *What?* (1973) is a mordant absurdist comedy made in the spirit of Roger Vadim and Terry Southern and loosely based on the themes of *Alice in Wonderland* and Henry James. The film is a rambling shaggy dog story about the sexual indignities that befall Nancy (Sydne Rome), a winsome young American hippie hitchhiking through Europe. After escaping a farcical rape attempt in the back of a truck, she soon finds herself stranded in the hothouse atmosphere of a remote Italian villa inhabited by a band of decadent, lecherous grotesques—the main trio are played by Marcello Mastrioanni, Hugh Griffith and Polanski himself. *What?* is also significant in that it is Polanski's only film to date in which a character breaks the fourth wall. The film was a failure with audiences and critics, although in the years since its release *What?* has attracted a minor cult following and a modicum of critical notice.

After filming Chinatown (1974) in Los Angeles, Polanski returned to Paris for his next film, *The Tenant* (1976), which was based on a 1964 novel by Roland Topor, a French writer of Polish-Jewish origin. In addition to directing the film, Polanski also played the lead role of Trelkovsky, a timid Polish immigrant living in Paris who seems to be possessed by the personality of a young woman who committed suicide by jumping out of the window from her apartment—the very apartment that Trelkovsky now occupies. Many have noted the similarities with *Repulsion* and *Rosemary's Baby*, and together with these two earlier works, *The Tenant* can be seen as the third installment in a loose trilogy of films called the "Apartment Trilogy" that explore the themes of social alienation and psychic and emotional breakdown. For *The Tenant*, Ingmar Bergman's regular cinematographer, Sven Nykvist, served as cameraman, and actors such as Isabelle Adjani, Shelley Winters, Melvyn Douglas and Jo Van Fleet appeared in supporting roles. French composer Philippe Sarde scored *The Tenant* and two future Polanski films, *Tess* and *Pirates*. In his autobiography, Polanski wrote: "I had a great admiration for American institutions and regarded the United States as the only truly democratic country in the world."

Polanski with wife Emmanuelle Seigner at the Cannes Film Festival

Unwilling to work in the United States after 1978 for fear of jail, Polanski continued to work in Europe. He dedicated his next film, *Tess* (1979), to the memory of his late wife, Sharon Tate. According to the director, after spending time with him in London in the summer of 1969, Tate left a copy of Thomas Hardy's *Tess of the d'Urbervilles* on Polanski's nightstand, along with a note suggesting that it would make a good film. *Tess* was Polanski's first film since his 1977 arrest in Los Angeles, and because of the American-British extradition treaty, *Tess* was shot in the north of France instead of Hardy's Dorset and Wiltshire; a replica of Stonehenge was constructed at Morienval for the final scene. Nastassja Kinski appeared in the title role opposite Peter Firth and Leigh Lawson. The film became the most expensive made in France up to that time, causing producer Claude Berri considerable anxiety when there was difficulty finding a North American distributor for the picture, which was nearly three hours long. Matters were also complicated when cinematographer Geoffrey Unsworth died in the middle of production and had to be replaced by Ghislain Cloquet. *Tess* was eventually released in North America by Columbia

Pictures, which had also distributed Polanski's earlier *Macbeth*. Ultimately, *Tess* proved a financial success and was well-received by both critics and the public. For *Tess*, Polanski won French César Awards for Best Picture and Best Director and received his fourth Academy Award nomination (and his second nomination for Best Director). The film received three Oscars: best cinematography, best art direction and best costume design. In addition, *Tess* was nominated for best picture (Polanski's second film to be nominated) and best original score.

Nearly seven years passed before Polanski completed his next film, *Pirates* (1986), a lavish period piece starring Walter Matthau, which the director intended as an homage to the beloved Errol Flynn swashbucklers of his childhood. *Pirates* was followed by *Frantic* (1988), a suspenseful thriller starring Harrison Ford and the actress/model Emmanuelle Seigner. She would go on to star in two more of his films, *Bitter Moon* (1992) and *The Ninth Gate* (1999).

Later work and honours

In 1997, Polanski directed a stage version of his 1967 film *The Fearless Vampire Killers*, a musical, which debuted on 4 October 1997 in Vienna as *Tanz der Vampire* (Dance of the Vampires), the German title of the film version. After closing in Vienna, the show had successful runs in Stuttgart, Hamburg, Berlin, and Budapest. On 11 March 1998, Polanski was elected a member of the Académie des Beaux-Arts.

Polanski at the 2002 Cannes Film Festival

In 2002, Polanski's production company, R.P. Productions, released *The Pianist*, an adaptation of the World War II autobiography of the same name by Polish-Jewish musician Władysław Szpilman. Szpilman's experiences as a persecuted Jew in Poland during WWII were reminiscent of Polanski and his family. While the fates of Szpilman and Polanski were to escape incarceration in any of the concentration camps, their family members did not, eventually perishing while captive during the course of the war. In May 2002, the film won the *Palme d'Or* (Golden Palm) award at the Cannes Film Festival, as well as Césars for Best Film and Best Director, and later the 2002 Academy Award for Directing. Because he would have been arrested once in the United States, Polanski did not attend the Academy Awards ceremony in Hollywood. After the announcement of the Best Director Award, Polanski received a standing ovation from most of those present in the theater. He later received the Crystal Globe award for outstanding artistic contribution to world cinema at the Karlovy Vary International Film Festival in 2004.

Late in 2004, Polanski directed a new film adaptation of the Charles Dickens' novel *Oliver Twist*, based on Ronald Harwood's screenplay. The shooting location was located at the Barrandov Studios in

Prague, Czech Republic and starred Barney Clark (as Oliver Twist), Harry Eden (as the Artful Dodger), Ben Kingsley (as Fagin) and Edward Hardwicke (as Mr. Brownlow). Polanski gathered a few previous collaborators from *The Pianist*—Ronald Harwood for the screenplay, Allan Starski as production designer and Pawel Edelman as director of photography. An attempt to adapt Robert Harris' *Pompeii* was abandoned in 2009.

In September 2009 Polanski was awarded a lifetime achievement "Golden Icon Award" by the Zurich Film Festival, which he was travelling to receive when he was arrested on 26 September.

Prior to his September 2009 arrest in Switzerland, Polanski was in production directing an adaptation of Harris' novel about a writer who stumbles upon a secret while ghosting the autobiography of a former British prime minister. The cast includes Ewan McGregor as the writer and Pierce Brosnan as prime minister Adam Lang. *The Ghost Writer* was co-produced as of February 2009 by Polanski's R.P Productions and Babelsberg Studios. The film was shot on locations in Germany. When his film premiered at the 60th Berlinale in February 2010, Polanski won a Silver Bear for Best Director. Unable to personally receive the prize, Polanski nevertheless mused, "Even if I could, I wouldn't, because the last time I went to a festival to get a prize I ended up in jail."

Personal life

Relationships

Polanski's first wife, Barbara Lass (née Kwiatkowska), was a Polish actress who also starred in Polanski's 1959 *When Angels Fall*. The couple were married in 1959 and divorced in 1961.

Martin Ransohoff introduced Polanski and rising actress Sharon Tate shortly before filming *The Fearless Vampire Killers*, and during the production the two of them began dating. On 20 January 1968, Polanski married Sharon Tate in London. In his autobiography, Polanski described his brief time with Tate as the best years of his life. This marriage ended with the death of Tate in the Manson murders, leaving Polanski devastated.

In 1976, Polanski started a romantic relationship with Nastassja Kinski, when she was 15 years old and he was 43 years old. In 1979, their relationship ended at the completion of filming Polanski's Oscar-nominated *Tess*, in which Kinski had played the lead role.

In 1989, Polanski and Emmanuelle Seigner married. They have two children, daughter Morgane and son Elvis. Polanski and his children speak Polish at home.

Sharon Tate's murder

Main article: Sharon Tate#Death and aftermath

Sharon Tate, Polanski's second wife, in *Eye of the Devil* (1967)

In 1969, Polanski and Tate were in London, as Polanski prepared for the film *The Day of the Dolphin*. Tate was pregnant and returned to Los Angeles in July, before her advanced pregnancy made travel impossible; Polanski remained in London and planned to join Tate before she was due to give birth in late August. Polanski asked his friend Wojciech Frykowski, and Frykowski's girlfriend, Abigail Folger to stay with Tate until his arrival.

On the night of 9 August 1969, Tate, Frykowski, Folger and two others were murdered at the Polanski residence. Polanski immediately returned to Los Angeles and was questioned by police who were satisfied that he was not involved in the murders. As the murders were particularly savage, and involved Hollywood celebrities, the case was widely reported throughout the United States and Europe. With little progress in the investigation, some sections of the media speculated that the murders had been a result of the victims' lifestyles, prompting Polanski to confront a group of journalists at a press conference and defend Tate and the other victims against "a multitude of slanders".

In December 1969, Charles Manson and several members of his "family" were arrested and subsequently charged with several murders, including that of Tate. Polanski returned to Europe. He later said that there was nothing to keep him in Hollywood and that to recover, he needed to find seclusion. Polanski has said that his absence on the night of the murders is the greatest regret of his life. In his autobiography, he wrote, "Sharon's death is the only watershed in my life that really matters", and commented that her murder changed his personality from a "boundless, untroubled sea of expectations and optimism" to one of "ingrained pessimism ... eternal dissatisfaction with life".

Sexual assault case

Main article: Roman Polanski sexual abuse case

On 11 March 1977, Polanski was arrested for the sexual assault of a 13-year-old, Samantha Geimer, that occurred the day before at the Hollywood home of actor Jack Nicholson. The girl testified before a grand jury that Polanski gave her both champagne and Quaalude, a sedative drug, and despite being asked to stop, he performed oral sex, intercourse and anal sex upon her. The grand jury returned an indictment charging him with "rape by use of drugs, perversion, sodomy, lewd and lascivious act upon a child under 14, and furnishing a controlled substance to a minor". At his arraignment Polanski pleaded not guilty to all charges.

In an effort to preserve her anonymity, Geimer's attorney arranged a plea bargain which Polanski accepted, and, under the terms, five charges from the indictment were to be dismissed. On 8 August 1977, Polanski entered a plea of guilty to Charge III of the indictment, "Unlawful Sexual Intercourse, in violation of California Penal Code § 261.5", a charge which is synonymous under California law with statutory rape. The judge, Laurence J. Rittenband, received a probation report and psychiatric evaluation, both indicating that Polanski should not serve jail time. In response, the filmmaker was ordered to a 90-day psychiatric evaluation at Chino State Prison.

On 28 January 1978, Polanski was released after undergoing the in-prison psychiatric evaluation, serving 42 days. Despite expectations and recommendations that he would receive only probation at sentencing, the judge "suggested to Polanski's attorneys" that more jail time and possible deportation were in order. Upon learning of the judge's plans Polanski fled to France on 1 February 1978, hours before he was to be formally sentenced. As a French citizen, he has been protected from extradition and has mostly lived in France, avoiding countries likely to extradite him. Because he fled prior to sentencing, all six of the original charges remain pending.

Geimer sued Polanski in 1988, alleging sexual assault, intentional infliction of emotional distress and seduction. In 1993 Polanski agreed to settle with Geimer; however, in August 1996 Polanski still owed her $604,416. Geimer and her lawyers would later confirm the settlement was completed. In 1997, Geimer publicly forgave Polanski and filed a formal request with the Los Angeles Police Department to drop charges against him. In 2003 she wrote an Op Ed piece in the Los Angeles Times advocating for him to be allowed to return to the US to accept an Academy Award.

On 26 September 2009, Polanski was taken into custody at the Zurich airport by Swiss police at the request of U.S. authorities, for a 2005 international arrest warrant, as he traveled to accept a lifetime achievement award at the Zurich Film Festival. After initially being jailed, on 4 December 2009 Polanski was granted house arrest at his Gstaad residence on US$4.5 million bail, while awaiting decision of appeals fighting extradition. On 22 January 2010, California Superior Court Judge Peter Espinoza ruled that Polanski must return to be sentenced.

On 12 July 2010, the Swiss authorities announced that they would not extradite Polanski to the U.S. in part due to a fault in the American request for extradition. Polanski was no longer subject to house arrest, or any monitoring by Swiss authorities. In a press conference held by Swiss Justice Minister Eveline Widmer-Schlumpf, she stated that Polanski's extradition to the U.S. was rejected, in part, because U.S. officials failed to produce certain documents, specifically "confidential testimony from a January 2010 hearing on Mr. Polanski's original sentencing agreement." According to Swiss officials, the records were required to determine if Polanski's 42-day court-ordered psychiatric evaluation at Chino State Prison constituted Polanski's whole sentence according to the now-deceased Judge Rittenband, reasoning that if this was the correct understanding, then "Roman Polanski would actually have already served his sentence and therefore both the proceedings on which the U.S. extradition request is founded and the request itself would have no foundation."

Vanity Fair libel case

In 2004, Polanski sued *Vanity Fair* magazine in London for libel. A 2002 article in the magazine written by A. E. Hotchner recounted a claim by Lewis H. Lapham, editor of *Harper's*, that Polanski had made sexual advances towards a young model as he was traveling to Sharon Tate's funeral, claiming that he could make her "the next Sharon Tate". The court permitted Polanski to testify via a video link, after he expressed fears that he might be extradited if he entered the United Kingdom. The trial started in July 2005 and Polanski made English legal history as the first claimant to give evidence by video link. During the trial, which included the testimony of Mia Farrow and others, it was claimed that the alleged scene at the famous New York City restaurant Elaine's could not have taken place on the date given, because Polanski only dined at this restaurant three weeks later. Also, the Norwegian model disputed accounts that he had claimed he could make her "the next Sharon Tate," saying Polanski had never spoken to her at all. In the course of the trial, Polanski stated that he had been unfaithful to Tate during their marriage. Polanski was awarded £50,000 damages by the High Court in London. Graydon Carter, editor of *Vanity Fair*, responded, "I find it amazing that a man who lives in France can sue a magazine that is published in America in a British courtroom".

Filmography

Director

Year	Film	Oscar nominations	Oscar wins
1955	*Zaczarowany rower* (also as *Bicycle*)		
1957	*Morderstwo* (also as *A Murderer*)		
	Uśmiech zębiczny (also as *A Toothful Smile*)		
	Rozbijemy zabawę (also as *Break Up the Dance*)		
1958	*Dwaj ludzie z szafą* (also as *Two Men and a Wardrobe*)		
1959	*Lampa* (also as *The Lamp*)		
	Gdy spadają anioły (also as *When Angels Fall*)		
1961	*Le Gros et le maigre* (also as *The Fat and the Lean*)		
	Ssaki (also as *Mammals*)		
1962	*Nóż w wodzie* (also as *Knife in the Water*)	1	
1964	*Les plus belles escroqueries du monde* (also as *The Beautiful Swindlers*)—segment: "La rivière de diamants"		
1965	*Repulsion**		

Year	Title		
1966	*Cul-de-Sac*		
1967	*The Fearless Vampire Killers or: Pardon Me, Madam, but Your Teeth Are in My Neck* (also as *Dance of the Vampires*)		
1968	*Rosemary's Baby**	2	1
1971	*The Tragedy of Macbeth*		
1973	*What?* (also as *Diary of Forbidden Dreams*)		
1974	*Chinatown*	11	1
1976	*Le Locataire* (also as *The Tenant*)*		
1979	*Tess*	6	3
1986	*Pirates*	1	
1988	*Frantic*		
1992	*Bitter Moon*		
1994	*Death and the Maiden*		
1999	*The Ninth Gate*		
2002	*The Pianist*	7	3
2005	*Oliver Twist*		
2007	*To Each His Own Cinema* (segment *Cinéma erotique*)		
2010	*The Ghost Writer*	The Oscar Nominations for 2010 are not yet known.	The Oscar Winners for 2010 are not yet known.

*These movies are part of his 'Apartment Trilogy'.

Actor

This list contains both cameos and more major roles.

- *Trzy opowieści* (aka *Three Stories*) as Genek 'The Little' (segment "Jacek", 1953)
- *Zaczarowany rower* (aka *Magical Bicycle*) as Adas (1955)
- *Rower* (aka *Bicycle*) as the Boy who wants to buy a bicycle (1955)
- *Pokolenie* (aka *A Generation*) as Mundek (1955)
- *Nikodem Dyzma* as the Boy at Hotel (1956)
- *Wraki* (aka *The Wrecks*, 1957)
- *Koniec nocy* (aka *End of the Night*) as the Little One (1957)
- *Dwaj ludzie z szafą* (aka *Two Men and a Wardrobe*) as the Bad boy (1958)

- *Zadzwońcie do mojej żony?* (aka *Call My Wife*) as a Dancer (1958)
- *Gdy spadają anioły* (aka *When Angels Fall Down*) as an Old woman (1959)
- *Lotna* as a Musician (1959)
- *Zezowate szczęście* (aka *Bad Luck*) as Jola's Tutor (1960)
- *Do widzenia, do jutra* (aka *Good Bye, Till Tomorrow*) as Romek (1960)
- *Niewinni czarodzieje* (aka *Innocent Sorcerers*) as Dudzio (1960)
- *Ostrożnie, Yeti!* (aka *Beware of Yeti!*, 1961)
- *Gros et le maigre, Le* (aka *The Fat and the Lean*) as The Lean (1961)
- *Samson* (1961)
- *Nóż w wodzie* (aka *Knife in the Water*) voice of Young Boy (1962)
- *Repulsion* as Spoon Player (1965)
- *The Fearless Vampire Killers* as Alfred, Abronsius' Assistant (1967)
- *The Magic Christian* as Solitary drinker (1969)
- *What?* as Mosquito (1972)
- *Chinatown* as Man with Knife (1974)
- *Blood for Dracula* (Andy Warhol) as Man in Tavern (1976)
- *Locataire, Le* (aka *The Tenant*) as Trelkovsky (1976)
- *Chassé-croisé* (1982)
- *En attendant Godot* (TV) as Lucky (1989)
- *Back in the USSR* as Kurilov (1992)
- *Una pura formalità* (aka *A Pure Formality*) as Inspector (1994)
- *Grosse fatigue* (aka *Dead Tired*) as Roman Polanski (1994)
- *Hommage à Alfred* (aka *Tribute to Alfred Lepetit*, 2000)
- *Zemsta* (aka *The Revenge*) as Papkin (2002)
- *Rush Hour 3* as Detective Revi (2007)
- *Caos Calmo* as Steiner (2007)

Writer

- Script for *A Day at the Beach* (1970) based on the 1962 novel of the same name by Simon Heere Heeresma.
- Polanski's autobiography, *Roman by Polanski*, sometimes known as *Roman*.

Awards and nominations

Year	Award	Category	Result
1963	Academy of Motion Picture Arts and Sciences	Best Foreign Language Film (*Knife in the Water*)	Nominated
1965	Berlin Film Festival	Silver Berlin Bear-Extraordinary Jury Prize (*Repulsion*)	Won
1966	Berlin Film Festival	Golden Bear (*Cul-de-Sac*)	Won
1968	Academy of Motion Picture Arts and Sciences	Best screenplay adaptation (*Rosemary's Baby*)	Nominated
1974	Academy of Motion Picture Arts and Sciences	Academy Award for Best Director (*Chinatown*)	Nominated
1974	Golden Globe Awards	Golden Globe Award for Best Director - Motion Picture (*Chinatown*)	Won
1974	British Academy of Film and Television Arts	Best Direction (*Chinatown*)	Won
1979	César Awards	César Award for Best Picture (*Tess*)	Won
1979	César Awards	César Award for Best Director (*Tess*)	Won
1979	Academy of Motion Picture Arts and Sciences	Academy Award for Directing (*Tess*)	Nominated
1979	Golden Globe Awards	Golden Globe Award for Best Foreign Film (*Tess*)	Won
1979	Golden Globe Awards	Golden Globe Award for Best Director—Motion Picture (*Tess*)	Nominated
2002	Cannes Film Festival *Palme d'Or* (Golden Palm)	Best film (*The Pianist*)	Won
2002	Academy of Motion Picture Arts and Sciences	Academy Award for Best Director (*The Pianist*)	Won
2002	*Académie des Arts et Techniques du Cinéma*	César Award for Best Film (*The Pianist*)	Won
2002	*Académie des Arts et Techniques du Cinéma*	Cesar Award for Best Director (*The Pianist*)	Won
2004	Karlovy Vary International Film Festival	Crystal Globe for outstanding artistic contribution to world cinema	Won
2009	Zurich Film Festival Golden Icon Award	Lifetime achievement	Won
2010	Berlin Film Festival	Silver Bear for Best Director (The Ghost Writer)	Won

References

Bibliography

- Bugliosi, Vincent, with Gentry, Kurt, (1974) *Helter Skelter, The Shocking Story of the Manson Murders*, Arrow, London. ISBN 0099975009
- Cronin, Paul (2005) *Roman Polanski: Interviews*, Mississippi: University Press of Mississippi. 200p
- Farrow, Mia (1997). *What Falls Away: A Memoir*, New York: Bantam.
- Feeney, F.X. (text); Duncan, Paul (visual design). (2006). *Roman Polanski*, Koln: Taschen. ISBN 3-8228-2542-5
- Jacke, Andreas (2010): *Roman Polanski—Traumatische Seelenlandschaften*, Gießen: Psychosozial-Verlag. ISBN 9783837920376, ISBN 9783837920376
- Kael, Pauline, *5001 Nights At The Movies*, Zenith Books, 1982. ISBN 0-09-933550-6
- King, Greg, *Sharon Tate and The Manson Murders*, Barricade Books, New York, 2000. ISBN 1-56980-157-6
- Leaming, Barbara (1981). *Polanski, The Filmmaker as Voyeur: A Biography*. New York: Simon & Schuster. ISBN 0671249851.
- Parker, John (1994). *Polanski*. London: Victor Gollancz Ltd. ISBN 0575056150.
- Polanski, Roman (1973) *Roman Polanski's What? From the original screenplay*, London: Lorrimer. 91p. ISBN 0856470333
- Polanski, Roman (1973) *What?*, New York: Third press, 91p, ISBN 089388121X
- Polanski, Roman (1975) *Three film scripts: Knife in the water* [original screenplay by Jerzy Skolimowski, Jakub Goldberg and Roman Polanski; translated by Boleslaw Sulik]; *Repulsion* [original screenplay by Roman Polanski and Gerard Brach]; *Cul-de-sac* [original screenplay by Roman Polanski and Gerard Brach], *introduction by Boleslaw Sulik, New York: Fitzhenry and Whiteside, 275p, ISBN 0064300625*
- Polanski, Roman (1984) *Knife in the water, Repulsion and Cul-de-sac: three filmscripts by Roman Polanski*, London: Lorrimer, 214p, ISBN 0856470511 (hbk) ISBN 0856470929 (pbk)
- Polanski, Roman (1984, 1985) *Roman by Polanski*, New York: Morrow. ISBN 0688026214, London: Heinemann. London: Pan. 456p. ISBN 0434591807 (hbk) ISBN 0330285971 (pbk)
- Polanski, Roman (2003) *Le pianiste*, Paris: Avant-Scene, 126p, ISBN 2847250166
- Visser, John J. 2008 *Satan-el: Fallen Mourning Star (Chapter 5)*. Covenant People's Books. ISBN 978-0-557-03412-3

External links

- Roman Polanski [1] at the Internet Movie Database
- Roman Polanski's official webpage [2]

Video links

- Additional CBS videos [3]
- Interview with Charlie Rose [4], March 2000
1. REDIRECT Template:Navboxes

Philippe Forquet

Philippe Forquet Viscount de Dorne born September 27, 1940 in Paris, France, is an actor and the son of a wealthy aristocrat, Marcius Forquet Viscount de Dorne.

Philippe Forquet made his film debut in 1960 in *La Menace* while still an art student and over the next few years became popular in France. Highly regarded for his appearance he was expected to make a successful transition into American films, after appearing opposite Jean Seberg in the film *In the French Style* (1963). Filmed in France, the film told of an American student (Seberg) who falls in love with an aristocrat (Forquet) while visiting France. It proved popular with both European and American audiences and Forquet travelled to Hollywood to work for 20th Century Fox. He was touted as the handsomest new actor in Hollywood, a cross between Montgomery Clift and Louis Jourdan.

He co-starred with Sandra Dee in *Take Her, She's Mine* as her romantic interest, and while the film was popular, it did not lead to other projects. During this time Forquet became engaged to the American actress Sharon Tate, however the relationship ended. He returned to France where his popularity had started to wane although he continued acting in television throughout the 1970s, also returning the United States to film *The Young Rebels* in 1971.

He was married to the American fashion model and actress Linda Morand, from 1970 until their divorce in 1976. He now lives in the town of Saint-Quentin, France where he took over his father's estate and the family business. He is re-married and has three children.

External links

- Philippe Forquet [1] at the Internet Movie Database

Doris Tate

Doris Tate	
Doris Tate in 1984, confronting Charles Watson at his parole hearing with the presentation of her victim's impact statement.	
Born	Doris Gwendolyn Willett January 16, 1924 Houston, Texas
Died	July 10, 1992 (aged 68) Los Angeles, California
Spouse	Paul Tate
Children	3 Daughters: Sharon Tate, Debra Tate, Patricia Tate

Doris Gwendolyn Tate (January 16, 1924 – July 10, 1992) was an American campaigner for the rights of crime victims. After the murder of her daughter, the actress Sharon Tate, and several others, she worked to raise public awareness about the United States corrections system and was influential in the amendment of California laws relating to the victims of violent crime.

Born in Houston, Texas, Tate was a housewife and mother of three daughters. In 1969, her eldest daughter, Sharon, was at the beginning of a film career, and married to film director Roman Polanski. Eight months pregnant with their first child, Tate and four others were murdered at the Polanski's Beverly Hills home in a case that was sensationalized throughout the world. The killers were eventually identified as Charles 'Tex' Watson, Susan Atkins and Patricia Krenwinkel, acting on behalf of the leader of their group, Charles Manson. All four were found guilty of the murders and sentenced to death, along with Leslie Van Houten, who had not participated in the murder of the Tate victims, but had participated in the murder of a Los Angeles couple the following night. The death sentences were overturned before they could be applied when the State of California temporarily abolished the death penalty.

For more than a decade after the murders, Tate battled depression and was withdrawn and unable to discuss her daughter's death. In 1982 she was told that Leslie Van Houten had obtained 300 signatures supporting her quest to achieve parole. Tate mounted a public campaign against Van Houten, winning the support of the National Enquirer, which printed coupons in its magazine for people to sign and send to Doris Tate. With more than 350,000 signatures, Tate demonstrated that a considerable number of people opposed Van Houten's parole, which was denied.

Tate then appeared on various television talk shows, discussing her opinion of the corrections system and the impact her daughter's murder had had on her family. She joined the Los Angeles chapter of the "Parents of Murdered Children" organization, and while she drew support from the group, also found that she was rewarded by assuming the role of counsellor. She later became an active member of the Victim Offender Reconciliation and Justice for Homicide Victims groups. She founded COVER, the Coalition on Victim's Equal Rights, and served on the California State Advisory Committee on Correctional Services as a victims' representative.

She was part of a group that worked toward the passage of Proposition 8, the Victim's Rights Bill, which was passed in 1982. It allowed the presentation of victim impact statements during the sentencing of violent attackers. Tate became the first Californian to make such a statement after the law was passed, when she spoke at the parole hearing of one of her daughter's killers.

In 1984 she ran for the California State Assembly as an advocate for victim's rights. Though unsuccessful, she continued to campaign for changes to existing laws, and was involved in the passage of Proposition 89, which allowed the governor of the state to overturn decisions made by the Board of Prison Terms.

Tate's assessment of Manson, Watson, Atkins, Krenwinkel and Van Houten was that their crimes were so vicious as to warrant execution. Addressing Charles Watson at his 1984 parole hearing, she said, "What mercy, Sir, did you show my daughter when she was begging for her life? What mercy did you show my daughter when she said give me two weeks to have my baby and then you can kill me? ... When will Sharon come up for parole?... Will these seven victims and possibly more walk out of their graves if you get paroled? You cannot be trusted." She confronted Watson again at his 1990 parole hearing.

Doris Tate's health began to deteriorate after she was diagnosed with a brain tumour. In 1992, she was one of several volunteer workers recognized by President George H. W. Bush as one of a "Thousand Points of Light." The ceremony, during which Tate and her family were honored by the President for their work in promoting victims' rights, marked Tate's final public appearance. She died later that year at the age of 68.

Her work was taken over by her younger daughter, Patti, who was involved in the establishment of the Doris Tate Crime Victims Bureau, a non-profit organization with the aim of monitoring criminal legislation and raising public awareness. The Bureau began in Sacramento, California in July, 1993. In 1995, the Doris Tate Crime Victims Foundation was established with the aim of providing assistance to victims and their families. Patti began to represent the Tate family at parole hearings for Manson and the other killers until 2000, when she died from breast cancer. Her role was assumed by the middle Tate daughter, Debra.

See also

- List of notable brain tumor patients

References

- King, Greg. *Sharon Tate and the Manson Murders* 2000. Barricade Books. ISBN 1-56980-157-6.

External links

- Doris Tate Crime Victims Bureau [1]
- Doris Tate Crime Victims Foundation [2]
- Doris Tate [3] at Find a Grave
- Sharon Tate's official website detailing Doris Tate's work [4]

Professional Career – Filmography

Barabbas (1961 film)

Barabbas is also the title of an 1893 book by Marie Corelli.

Barabbas	
Theatrical release poster	
Directed by	Richard Fleischer
Produced by	Dino De Laurentiis Luigi Luraschi
Written by	Pär Lagerkvist (Novel) Nigel Balchin Diego Fabbri Christopher Fry
Starring	Anthony Quinn Silvana Mangano Katy Jurado Arthur Kennedy Harry Andrews Ernest Borgnine Vittorio Gassman Jack Palance
Music by	Mario Nascimbene
Cinematography	Aldo Tonti
Editing by	Alberto Gallitti Raymond Poulton
Distributed by	Columbia Pictures
Release date(s)	December 23, 1961 (Italy) October 10, 1962 (US)
Running time	144 minutes
Country	Italy
Language	English

Barabbas is a 1961 film expanding on the career of Barabbas, from the Christian Passion narrative in the *Gospel of Mark* and other gospels. It starred Anthony Quinn as Barabbas, with Silvana Mangano, Katy Jurado, Arthur Kennedy, Harry Andrews, Ernest Borgnine, Vittorio Gassman, and Jack Palance, and was distributed by Columbia Pictures. The film, conceived as a grand Roman epic, was based on the Nobel-Prize winning novel *Barabbas* (1950) by Pär Lagerkvist. A previous film version of the novel, in Swedish, had been made in 1953.

The film of Lagerkvist's novel was directed by Richard Fleischer and shot in Rome under the supervision of producer Dino De Laurentiis. It included many spectacular scenes, including a battle of gladiators in a Cinecittà mock-up of the Colosseum, and a final crucifixion shot during a real eclipse of the sun.

The music score by Mario Nascimbene contained a stark experimental component—what the composer himself called 'new sounds', in order to demonstrate the eclipse as a supernatural event in the Judean age (see liner notes of CD of original soundtracks of *Alexander the Great* and *Barabbas*, music composed, orchestrated and conducted by Mario Nascimbene).

Plot

Shortly before the crucifixion of Christ, Pontius Pilate (Arthur Kennedy) offers to release either Jesus Christ or Barabbas in keeping with the local custom. As the Bible story goes, Barabbas is the one the crowd chooses.

Barabbas leaves and returns to his friends. His friends are glad to see him, but Barabbas wants to know where his lover Rachel is (Silvana Mangano). They inform him that Rachel had changed while he was away, and was following the teachings of Christ. Rachel soon returns, but she is not overjoyed to see Barabbas again. During their reunion Christ is crucified. As Christ dies the sky turns dark. Shaken by this, Barabbas goes to witness the crucifixion. Afterwards he goes to witness Christ being sealed in the tomb. On the third morning Barabbas goes to the tomb to find the tomb open, and Christ gone. Rachel tells him that Christ has risen, but Barabbas dismisses this as illusion, or that his followers had taken his body. He goes to see the apostle Peter and Christ's other followers to demand what happened to the body - they do not know where he is but do believe he is risen. Rachel begins to teach others in Jerusalem about Christ and an impending, fiery end of the world. Soon, Rachel's teachings lead to her being stoned to death by the same men who had Jesus crucified. When Barabbas comes across them later while robbing a caravan, he assaults one of the men. For this, Barabbas is arrested by the Roman authorities. Pilate decides not to execute Barabbas, but instead sentences him to a life sentence in the sulfur mines of Sicily.

Barabbas is taken to the sulfur mines of Sicily - where the medallion designating him the property of the Emperor is placed around his neck. He manages to survive a hellish existence for the next 20 years in the mines. Eventually he is chained to Sahek (Vittorio Gassman), who was sent to the mines in punishment for letting slaves escape. Sahek was also a Christian - and had carved a cross on the back of his medallion. At first Sahek hates him, but the two men eventually become friends. After some time Sahek becomes too weak to work, and is about to be killed - but the mine is destroyed in an earthquake. Sahek and Barabbas are the only survivors. After they recover from their injuries they are sent to the fields to work. As the only survivors of the disaster, they catch the eye of the wife of the local prefect - who is due to leave for Rome to become a Senator. She insists that they be brought along for luck.

Once in Rome the men are trained to become gladiators by Torvald (Jack Palance) - the top gladiator in Rome. Just after one of the gladiatorial events Sahek is overheard speaking about his faith in Christ's sacrificial death, and the renovation of the world by God's fire, and he is executed by Torvald for treason. The next day Torvald and Barabbas battle in the Colosseum, with Barabbas winning. Impressed with Barabbas, the Roman Emperor Nero sets him free. Barabbas recovers the remains of Sahek, and takes his body to the catacombs, where the local Christians are worshiping, for a proper burial.

Barabbas is separated from the Christians within the catacombs, and becomes lost while trying to find his way out. When he eventually emerges from the catacombs, Rome is on fire. Upon entering the city, Barabbas is told that the Christians started the fire. Believing that the end of the world has come (as he had heard Rachel and Sahek teaching), Barabbas begins to set aflame more buildings. Barabbas is confronted by Roman soldiers and he tells them that he is a follower of Christ. Barabbas is imprisoned with several other Christians, one of whom is Peter. Peter corrects Barabbas' mistaken intentions of burning Rome. Afterwards, the Christians are executed en masse by crucifixion, in the persecutions that followed the fire. Throughout his life Barabbas was reputed as the man who could not die; having finally placed faith in Christ, he dies.

External links

- *Barabbas* [1] at the Internet Movie Database
- *Barabbas* [2] at Allmovie

Hemingway's Adventures of a Young Man

Hemingway's Adventures of a Young Man	
Directed by	Martin Ritt
Produced by	Jerry Wald
Written by	A.E. Hotchner (screenplay) Ernest Hemingway (stories)
Starring	Richard Beymer
Music by	Franz Waxman
Cinematography	Lee Garmes
Editing by	Hugh S. Fowler
Distributed by	Twentieth Century-Fox Film Corporation
Release date(s)	1962
Running time	145 minutes
Country	United States
Language	English

Hemingway's Adventures of a Young Man is a 1962 drama film directed by Martin Ritt based on the Nick Adams stories by Ernest Hemingway, and featuring Richard Beymer as Adams.

Cast

- Richard Beymer as Nick Adams
- Diane Baker as Carolyn
- Corinne Calvet as Contessa
- Fred Clark as Mr. Turner
- Dan Dailey as Billy Campbell
- James Dunn as Telegrapher
- Juano Hernández as Bugs
- Arthur Kennedy as Dr. Adams
- Ricardo Montalbán as Major Padula
- Paul Newman as The Battler
- Susan Strasberg as Rosanna
- Jessica Tandy as Mrs. Adams
- Eli Wallach as John

- Edward Binns as Brakeman
- Philip Bourneuf as City Editor
- Tullio Carminati as Rosanna's Father
- Marc Cavell as Eddy Boulton
- Charles Fredericks as Mayor
- Simon Oakland as Joe Boulton
- Michael J. Pollard as George
- Whit Bissell as Ludstrum
- Lillian Adams as Indian Woman
- Walter Baldwin as Conductor
- Laura Cornell as Headwaiter
- Laura Cornell as Burlesque Queen
- Miriam Golden as Indian Mid-Wife
- Pitt Herbert as Bartender
- Pat Hogan as Billy Tabeshaw
- Baruch Lumet as Morris
- Burt Mustin as Old Soldier
- Sherry Staiger as Burlesque Queen
- Sharon Tate as Burlesque Queen
- Alfredo Varelli as Father Ben
- Mel Welles as Italian Sergeant

External links

- *Hemingway's Adventures of a Young Man* [1] at the Internet Movie Database
- *Hemingway's Adventures of a Young Man* [2] at Allmovie

The Americanization of Emily

The Americanization of Emily	
original film poster	
Directed by	Arthur Hiller
Produced by	Martin Ransohoff
Written by	William Bradford Huie *(novel)* Paddy Chayefsky *(screenplay)*
Starring	James Garner Julie Andrews Melvyn Douglas
Music by	Johnny Mandel
Cinematography	Philip H. Lathrop Christopher Challis
Editing by	Tom McAdoo
Distributed by	MGM
Release date(s)	27 October 1964
Running time	115 minutes
Country	United States
Language	English

The Americanization of Emily is a 1964 American comedy-drama war film directed by Arthur Hiller and written by Paddy Chayefsky, loosely adapted from the novel of the same name by William Bradford Huie. Set in London in 1944 during World War II, in the weeks leading up to D-Day, the black-and-white film stars James Garner, Julie Andrews and Melvyn Douglas and features James Coburn, Joyce Grenfell and Keenan Wynn. Both Garner and Andrews consider it their favorite of the films they appeared in.

Plot

LCDR Charlie Madison (James Garner), USNR, is a cynical and highly efficient adjutant to RADM William Jessup (Melvyn Douglas) in London. Madison's job as a dog robber is to keep his boss and other high-ranking officers supplied with luxury goods and amiable Englishwomen. He falls in love with a driver from the motor pool, Emily Barham (Julie Andrews), who has lost her husband, brother, and father in the war. Madison's sybaritic, "American" lifestyle amid wartime scarcity both fascinates and disgusts Emily, but she does not want to lose another loved one to war and finds the "practicing coward" Madison irresistible.

Under stress since the death of his wife, Jessup obsesses over the Army and its Air Corps overshadowing the Navy in the forthcoming D-Day invasion. The mentally unstable admiral decides that "The first dead man on Omaha Beach must be a sailor." A film will document the death, and the casualty will be buried in a "Tomb of the Unknown Sailor."

Despite his best efforts to avoid the duty Madison and his gung-ho friend, LCDR "Bus" Cummings (James Coburn), find themselves and a film crew with the combat engineers who will be the first on shore. When Madison tries to retreat to safety, Cummings forces him forward with a pistol. A German shell lands near Madison, making him the first American to die on Omaha Beach. Hundreds of newspaper and magazine covers reprint a photograph of Madison on the shore, making him a martyr. Jessup, having recovered from his breakdown, regrets his part in Madison's death but plans to use it in support of the Navy when testifying before a Senate committee in Washington. Losing another man she loves to the war devastates Emily.

Then comes unexpected news: Madison is not dead, but alive and well in an English hospital. A relieved Jessup now plans to show him during the Senate testimony as the heroic "first man on Omaha Beach". Madison, angry about his senseless near-death, uncharacteristically plans to act nobly by telling the world the truth of what happened on the beach, even if it means being imprisoned for cowardice. Emily convinces him to instead choose happiness with her by keeping quiet and accepting his heroic role.

Cast

- James Garner as Lt. Cmdr. Charles E. "Charlie" Madison
- Julie Andrews as Emily Barham
- Melvyn Douglas as Admiral William Jessup
- James Coburn as Lt. Cmdr. Paul "Bus" Cummings
- Joyce Grenfell as Mrs. Barham
- Keenan Wynn as Old Sailor
- Edward Binns as Admiral Thomas Healy
- Liz Fraser as Sheila
- William Windom as Captain Harry Spaulding
- John Crawford as Chief Petty Officer Paul Adams
- Douglas Henderson as Captain Marvin Ellender
- Edmon Ryan as Admiral Hoyle
- Steve Franken as Young Sailor
- Alan Sues as Petty Officer Enright
- Sharon Tate had an uncredited role as "Beautiful Girl".

Soundtrack

The film introduced the song "Emily", composed by Johnny Mandel with lyrics by Johnny Mercer, performed by Julie Andrews. The song was later recorded by Barbra Streisand for *The Movie Album* (2003).

Awards nominations

The film was nominated for two Academy Awards:

- Academy Award for Best Art Direction - (George W. Davis, Hans Peters, Elliot Scott, Henry Grace, Robert R. Benton)
- Academy Award for Best Cinematography – (Philip H. Lathrop)
- BAFTA Award for Best Actress – (Julie Andrews)

Comparison with the novel

The movie is based on William Bradford Huie's 1959 book of the same name.

The New York Times ran a brief news item mention of William Bradford Huie's novel prior to its publication, but never reviewed the novel, although in 1963 Paddy Chayefsky's development of the novel into a screenplay was found worthy of note.

Chayefsky's adaptation, while retaining the title, characters, situation, background and many specific plot incidents, nevertheless told a very different story. "I found the book, which is serious in tone, essentially a funny satire, and that's how I'm treating it."

The screenplay's theme of cowardice as a virtue has no parallel in the novel; in fact, the novel does not mention cowardice at all.

The screenplay implies, but never explicitly explains what is meant by the term "Americanization." The novel uses "Americanized" to refer to a woman who accepts, as a normal condition of wartime, the exchange of her sexual favors for gifts of rare wartime commodities. Thus, in reply to the question "has Pat been Americanized," a character answers:

> "Thoroughly. She carries a diaphragm in her kitbag. She has seen the ceilings of half the rooms in the Dorchester [hotel]. She asks that it be after dinner: she doesn't like it on an empty stomach. She admits she's better after steak than after fish. She requires that it be in a bed, and that the bed be in Claridge's, the Savoy, or the Dorchester."

This theme runs throughout the novel. Another character says "We operate just like a whorehouse... except we don't sell it for cash. We swap it for Camels and nylons and steak and eggs and lipstick... this dress... came from Saks Fifth Avenue in the diplomatic pouch." Emily asks Jimmy "am I behaving like a whore?" Jimmy's reply is: "Whoring is a peacetime activity."

The screenplay uses Hershey bars to symbolize the luxuries enjoyed by Americans and their "Americanized' companions; the novel uses strawberries rather than chocolate bars, in a parallel way. In his first dinner with Emily, he orders the waiter to bring strawberries. "She protested that they were too forbidden, too expensive." Jimmy convinces her to accept them by arguing that "If you don't eat them, they'll be eaten by one of these expense-account correspondents." Later, she asks Jimmy, "If I fall in love with you, how can I know whether I love you for yourself or for the strawberries?"

The novel briefly mentions that Emily's mother, Mrs. Barham, has been mentally affected by wartime stress, but she is not a major character. There is no mention of her self-deception or pretense that her husband and son are still alive. The movie contains a long scene between Charlie and Mrs. Barham, full of eloquent antiwar rhetoric, in which Charlie breaks down Mrs. Barham's denial and reduces her to tears while nevertheless insisting that he has performed an act of kindness. The novel has no parallel to this scene.

In the movie, Charlie is comically unprepared to make the documentary movie demanded by Admiral Jessup, and is assisted only a bumbling and drunken serviceman played by Keenan Wynn. In the book, Charlie has, in fact, been a PR professional in civilian life, takes the assignment seriously, and leads a team of competent cinematographers.

External links

- *The Americanization of Emily* [1] at the Internet Movie Database
- *The Americanization of Emily* [2] at the TCM Movie Database
- *The Americanization of Emily* [3] at Allmovie
- *The Americanization of Emily* [4] at Rotten Tomatoes
- James Garner Interview on the *Charlie Rose Show* [5]
- James Garner interview [6] at Archive of American Television

Eye of the Devil

Eye of the Devil	
 from the film's trailer	
Directed by	J. Lee Thompson
Produced by	John Calley, Martin Ransohoff
Written by	Philip Loraine (novel — *Day of the Arrow*), Robin Estridge, Dennis Murphy
Starring	Deborah Kerr, David Niven, Donald Pleasence, David Hemmings, Sharon Tate
Music by	Gary McFarland
Cinematography	Erwin Hillier
Editing by	Ernest Walter
Distributed by	Filmways Pictures, Metro-Goldwyn-Mayer
Release date(s)	1967
Running time	96 min.
Country	United Kingdom
Language	English

Eye of the Devil is a 1967 film with occult and supernatural themes. This film was set in rural France and filmed in England.

Synopsis

David Niven plays the owner of a vineyard, who is called back to the estate when it falls on hard times. Accompanied by his wife (Deborah Kerr), the couple are confronted by a beautiful witch (Sharon Tate), who also lives on the estate with her brother (David Hemmings). As time passes it becomes clear that a blood sacrifice is expected to return the vineyard to its former glory.

Filmed in 1965, it featured the first film performance of Tate, who was cast by Filmways executive Martin Ransohoff who hailed her as his great discovery. Finally released two years later it attracted little attention, however *The New York Times* wrote of Tate's "chillingly beautiful but expressionless" performance. Although it was not a commercial success in the United States when first released, it was popular in Europe, and it has acquired a degree of cult status, largely due to its surreal themes, and the 1969 murder of Tate.

The film is also known by the titles *Thirteen* and *13*.

See also

- 1967 in film

External links

- *Eye of the Devil* [1] at the Internet Movie Database
- *Eye of the Devil* [2] at Allmovie

Don't Make Waves

Don't Make Waves	
original movie poster	
Directed by	Alexander Mackendrick
Produced by	John Calley Martin Ransohoff Ira Wallach
Starring	Tony Curtis Claudia Cardinale Sharon Tate Robert Webber
Cinematography	Philip H. Lathrop
Editing by	Rita Roland Thomas Stanford
Distributed by	Metro-Goldwyn-Mayer
Release date(s)	1967
Running time	97 min.

Don't Make Waves (1967) is a Metro-Goldwyn-Mayer sex farce (with elements of the beach party genre) which starred Tony Curtis, Claudia Cardinale and Sharon Tate. The film is based on the 1959 novel, *Muscle Beach*, by Ira Wallach, who also wrote the screenplay.

Directed by Alexander Mackendrick, the film depicted a series of romantic triangles between different groupings of the principal cast and supporting players among several backdrops involving Southern California culture (swimming pools, bodybuilding, beach life, fantastic real estate, mudslides, metaphysical gurus, etc.).

During the previous few years, films and pop music which related to California beach culture had proved very popular, although by the late 1960s, the popularity of Tony Curtis as a matinee idol was beginning to wane. In recent times the film has received more positive comments from reviewers, such as Leonard Maltin who describes it as "a gem", and makes note of the "fine direction and funny performance by Sharon Tate".

Music

The score was composed by Vic Mizzy. Jim McGuinn and Chris Hillman wrote the title song, "Don't Make Waves," performed by The Byrds over the opening credits.

Production notes

Sharon Tate told her husband Roman Polanski that her experience working on this film was not particularly enjoyable. The production atmosphere was tense, and it was worsened when an uncredited stuntman drowned when he parachuted into the Pacific Ocean.

The film was Sharon Tate's third to be produced, but as it was the first to be released in cinemas, it is generally considered to be her debut. MGM mounted an extensive publicity campaign upon its release that was based largely on Tate and her character, Malibu, and life-sized cardboard cutouts of Tate wearing a bikini were placed in cinema foyers throughout the United States. It was also linked to a widespread advertising campaign by *Coppertone* which also featured Tate, but the film received generally poor reviews and failed to achieve success at the box office.

The Malibu Barbie doll, first produced in 1973, was based on Tate and her character, Malibu.

Dave Draper, who plays Malibu's boyfriend Harry, was the 1965 IFBB Mr. America and the 1966 IFBB Mr. Universe.

1966 NABBA Mr. Universe bodybuilder Chester Yorton, who plays Ted Gunder, made one other film - in 1964's *Muscle Beach Party*, he plays the character named Hulk.

In *American Prince*, his 2009 autobiography, Tony Curtis wrote of making *Don't Make Waves*: "The plot was utterly ridiculous, but I agreed to appear in the film because I got a percentage of the gross."

Cast

Actors	Characters	info
Tony Curtis	Carlo Cofield	
Claudia Cardinale	Laura Califatti	
Sharon Tate	Malibu	
David Draper	Harry Hollard	
Joanna Barnes	Diane Prescott	
Robert Webber	Rod Prescott	
Reg Lewis	Monster	
Mort Sahl	Sam Lingonberry	
Edgar Bergen	Madame Lavinia	

Dub Taylor	Electrician	
Mary Grace Canfield	Seamstress	
Holly Haze	Myrna	
Sarah Selby	Ethyl	
Julie Payne	Helen	
Douglass Henderson	Henderson	
Chester Yorton	Ted Gunder	
Ann Elder	Millie Gunder	
Marc London	Fred Barker	
Paul Barselou	Pilot	as Paul Barselow
George Tyne	Newspaperman	
David Fresco	Newspaperman	
Gilbert Green	Newspaperman	as Gil Green
Eduardo Tirello	Decorator	
Jim Backus	Himself	uncredited
Henny Backus	Herself	uncredited
China Lee	Topless swimmer	uncredited
Joanne Hashimoto	Female Gymnast	uncredited

External links

- *Don't Make Waves* [1] at the Internet Movie Database
- *Don't Make Waves* [2] at Allmovie
- *Don't Make Waves* [3] at the TCM Movie Database
- Review of *Don't Make Waves* [4] at TVGuide.com

The Fearless Vampire Killers

The Fearless Vampire Killers	
film poster by Frank Frazetta	
Directed by	Roman Polanski
Produced by	Gene Gutowski
Written by	Roman Polanski Gérard Brach
Starring	Jack MacGowran, Roman Polanski, Sharon Tate, Ferdy Mayne
Music by	Krzysztof Komeda
Cinematography	Douglas Slocombe
Editing by	Alastair McIntyre
Distributed by	MGM
Release date(s)	🇬🇧 February, 1967 🇺🇸 November 13, 1967
Running time	91 min. 107 min. (Director's Cut)
Country	UK US
Language	English

The Fearless Vampire Killers (originally titled *Dance of the Vampires*) is a 1967 comedy horror film directed by Roman Polanski, written by Gérard Brach and Polanski, and produced by Gene Gutowski. It has been produced as a musical, named *Dance of the Vampires*.

Plot

This film takes us into the heart of Transylvania where Professor Abronsius, of the University of Königsberg, and his apprentice Alfred are on the hunt for vampires. Abronsius is old and withering and barely able to survive the cold ride through the wintry forests. Alfred is bumbling and introverted. The hunters come to a small Central European town seemingly at the end of a long search for signs of vampires. The two stay at a local inn, full of angst-ridden townspeople who perform strange rituals to fend off an unseen evil.

Whilst staying at the inn, Alfred develops a fondness for Sarah, the daughter of the tavern keeper Yoine Shagal. After witnessing Sarah being kidnapped by the vampire, Count von Krolock, the two follow his snow trail, leading them to Krolock's ominous castle in the snow-blanketed hills nearby. They break into the castle, but are trapped by the Count's hunchback servant, Koukol. Upon being taken to see the count, he affects an air of aristocratic dignity whilst he cleverly questions Abronsius about his interest in bats and why he has come to the castle. They also encounter the Count's son, the foppish (and homosexual) Herbert. Meanwhile, Shagal himself has been vampirized and sets on his plan to turn Magda, the tavern's beautiful maidservant, into his vampire bride.

Despite misgivings, Abronsius and Alfred accept the Count's invitation to stay in his ramshackle gothic castle, where Alfred spends the night fitfully. The next morning, Abronsius plans to find the castle crypt and kill the Count, seemingly forgetting about the fate of Sarah. The crypt is guarded by the hunchback, so after some wandering they climb in through a roof window. However, Abronsius gets stuck in the window and it is up to Alfred to kill the Count, which he feels unable to do. He has to go back outside to free Abronsius, on the way coming upon Sarah having a bath in her room. She seems oblivious to her danger when he pleads for her to come away with him.

After freeing Abronsius, who is half frozen, they re-enter the castle. Alfred again seeks Sarah but meets Herbert instead, who first attempts to seduce him and then, after Alfred realizes that Herbert's reflection does not show in the mirror, reveals his vampire nature and attempts to bite him. Abronsius and Alfred flee from Herbert through a dark stairway to safety, only to be trapped behind a locked door. They also realise night is falling. As they watch horrified, the gravestones below open up and they see that there are many vampires at the castle. The Count appears, mocking them and tells them their fate is sealed. He leaves them to attend a dance, where Sarah will be presented as the next vampire victim.

However, the hunters escape by boiling water in a cannon and blowing off the door, and come to the dance in disguise, where they grab Sarah and flee. Escaping by horse carriage, they are now unaware that it is too late for Sarah, who bites Alfred, thus allowing vampires to be released into the world.

Cast

- Jack MacGowran as Professor Abronsius
- Roman Polanski as Alfred, Abronsius's assistant
- Ferdy Mayne as Count von Krolock
- Iain Quarrier as Herbert von Krolock
- Terry Downes as Koukol, Krolock's servant
- Alfie Bass as Yoine Shagal, the innkeeper
- Jessie Robins as Rebecca Shagal
- Sharon Tate as Sarah Shagal
- Fiona Lewis as Magda, Shagal's maid

Production

Coming straight on the heels of Polanski's international success with *Repulsion*, the film was mounted on a lavish scale - color cinematography, huge sets in England, location filming in the Alps, elaborate costumes and choreography suitable for a period epic. Previously accustomed only to extremely low budgets, Polanski chose some of the finest English cinema craft artists to work on the film: cameraman Douglas Slocombe, production designer Wilfrid Shingleton. Polanski engaged noted choreographer Tutte Lemkow, who played the titular musician in *Fiddler on the Roof*, for the film's climactic danse macabre minuet.

During filming the director decided to switch formats to anamorphic while filming on location. Flat scenes already filmed were optically converted to match.

In his autobiography, Roman Polanski discusses some of the difficulties in filming *The Fearless Vampire Killers*: "Our first month's outdoor filming became a series of ingenious improvisations, mainly because the last-minute switch from one location (Austria) to another (Urtijëi, an Italian ski resort in the Dolomites) had left us so little time to revise our shooting schedules. The fact that we were filming in Italy entailed the employment of a certain number of Italian technicians, and that, in turn, bred some international friction. Gene Gutowski (the film's European producer) rightly suspected that the Italians were robbing us blind."[citation needed]

Despite numerous production headaches, Polanski is said to have enjoyed making the film. His cinematographer, Douglas Slocombe, was quoted by Ivan Butler in his book, *The Cinema of Roman Polanski*, as saying, "I think he (Roman) put more of himself into *Dance of the Vampires* than into another film. It brought to light the fairy-tale interest that he has. One was conscious all along when making the picture of a Central European background to the story. Very few of the crew could see anything in it - they thought it old-fashioned nonsense. But I could see this background....I have a French background myself, and could sense the Central European atmosphere that surrounds it. The figure of Alfred is very much like Roman himself - a slight figure, young and a little defenseless - a touch of Kafka. It is very much a personal statement of his own humour. He used to chuckle all the way through."[citation needed]

When the film was first released in the United States, MGM wanted to market it as a farce by saddling it with a longer title - **The Fearless Vampire Killers, or Pardon Me, But Your Teeth Are in My Neck**.[citation needed] The director was less than pleased. Over the years it has been reported in most sourcesWikipedia:Avoid weasel words that producer Martin Ransohoff was the culprit responsible for cutting *Dance of the Vampires* for the American release, but he was completely innocent of this.[citation needed] The film fell into the hands of MGM Supervising Editor Margaret Booth. Booth and MGM Head of Theatrical Post Production, Merle Chamberlain, made the cuts and remixed the film in an attempt to make it 'kooky and cartoony.'[citation needed]

Though it was critically panned on its initial release, *The Fearless Vampire Killers* has garnered latter-day praise Wikipedia:Avoid weasel words for its vivid atmosphere and audacious balance of broad comedy with Hammer Films-style horror.

This film was the source material for the wildly popular European stage musical *Tanz der Vampire*. It is peppered with numerous references to King Richard III of England, who even appears in the ball scene.

Director of Photography Douglas Slocombe would work with actor Ronald Lacey, who plays one of the villagers, again in the epic blockbuster film *Raiders of the Lost Ark* in 1981.

Style and themes

The Fearless Vampire Killers was Polanski's first feature to be photographed in color and using a widescreen 2.35:1 aspect ratio. The film's striking visual style, with its snow-covered, fairy-tale landscapes, recalls the work of Russian fantasy filmmakers Aleksandr Ptushko and Alexander Row.Wikipedia:No original research Similarly, the richly textured, moonlit-winter-blue color schemes of the village and the snowy valleys evoke the magical, kaleidoscopic paintings of the great Russian-Jewish artist Marc Chagall, after whom the innkeeper in the film is named.

The film is also notable in that it features Polanski's love of winter sports, particularly skiing. In this respect, *The Fearless Vampire Killers* recalls Polanski's earlier short film, *Ssaki*.

Soundtrack

The score was provided by Krzysztof Komeda, who also scored *Rosemary's Baby*.

External links

- *The Fearless Vampire Killers* [1] at the Internet Movie Database
- *The Fearless Vampire Killers* [2] at Allmovie
- *The Fearless Vampire Killers* [3] at the TCM Movie Database
- Review of The Fearless Vampire Killers [4]
- "The Fearless Vampire Killers: A Tale of Two Versions" *DVD Savant* [5]
- "The Fearless Vampire Killers Retrospective by Scott Hutchins" *Film Scope* [6]
- Review of Dance Of The Vampires [7]

Valley of the Dolls (film)

Valley of the Dolls	
Original film poster	
Directed by	Mark Robson
Produced by	David Weisbart
Written by	**Novel:** Jacqueline Susann **Screenplay:** Helen Deutsch Dorothy Kingsley Harlan Ellison (uncredited)
Starring	Barbara Parkins Patty Duke Sharon Tate Susan Hayward Lee Grant
Music by	André Previn & Dory Previn (songs) John Williams
Cinematography	William H. Daniels
Editing by	Dorothy Spencer
Distributed by	20th Century Fox
Release date(s)	December 15, 1967
Running time	123 min.
Country	United States
Language	English
Gross revenue	$44,432,255 (box office) $20,000,000 (rentals)

Valley of the Dolls is a 1967 American drama film based on the 1966 novel of the same name by Jacqueline Susann. The "dolls" within the title is a slang term for downers, mood-altering drugs. The film, which was produced by David Weisbart and directed by Mark Robson, received a great deal of publicity during its production. Upon release it was a commercial success, though universally panned by critics. It was re-released in 1969 following the murder of star Sharon Tate, and once again proved commercially viable. In the years since its production, it has come to be regarded as a camp classic.

Co-star Barbara Parkins, attending a July 1997 screening of the film at the Castro Theatre in San Francisco, told the sold-out crowd, "I know why you like it... because it's so bad!" The movie was remade in 1981 for television as *Jacqueline Susann's Valley of the Dolls*.

Plot

Three young women meet when they embark on the beginning of their careers. Neely O'Hara (Duke) is a plucky kid with undeniable talent who acts in a Broadway play, the legendary actress Helen Lawson (Hayward) is the star of the play, and Jennifer North (Tate), a beautiful blonde with limited talent, is in the chorus. Anne Welles (Parkins) is a New England ingenue who recently arrived in New York City and works for a theatrical agency that represents Helen Lawson. The three women become fast friends, sharing the bonds of ambition and the tendency to fall in love with the wrong men.

O'Hara becomes a major success and moves to Hollywood to pursue a lucrative film career, but almost immediately falls victim to the eponymous "dolls": prescription drugs, particularly the barbiturates Seconal and Nembutal and various stimulants. Her career is shattered by her erratic behavior and she is committed to a sanitarium.

Meanwhile, Jennifer follows Neely to Hollywood, where she marries nightclub singer Tony Polar (Scotti) and becomes pregnant. When she learns that he has the hereditary condition Huntington's chorea, a fact his domineering half-sister and manager Miriam (Grant) had been concealing, Jennifer has an abortion. Faced with Tony's mounting medical expenses, Jennifer finds herself working in French "art films" (extremely tame soft-core pornography) to pay the bills.

Anne, having become a highly successful model, also falls under the allure of "dolls" to escape her doomed relationship with cad Lyon Burke (Burke), who has an affair with Neely. Jennifer is diagnosed with breast cancer and told she must have a mastectomy. Jennifer places a call to her mother, to finally reach out to her, hoping for moral support. However, she receives a detached mother who is only concerned with the reaction from her friends upon Jennifer's "art films". Jennifer's mother also reminds Jennifer of the financial needs that she has placed on her daughter over the years. Faced with this, Jennifer succumbs to the depression that has haunted Jennifer's every step and she commits suicide with an overdose of "dolls". Neely is released from the sanitarium and given a chance to resurrect her career, but the attraction of "dolls" and alcohol proves too strong and she spirals into a hellish decline.

Anne abandons drugs and her unfaithful lover and returns to New England. Lyon Burke ends his affair with Neely and asks Anne to marry him, but she refuses.

Cast

- Barbara Parkins as Anne Welles
- Patty Duke as Neely O'Hara
- Sharon Tate as Jennifer North
- Paul Burke as Lyon Burke
- Tony Scotti as Tony Polar
- Susan Hayward as Helen Lawson
- Martin Milner as Mel Anderson
- Charles Drake as Kevin Gillmore
- Alexander Davion as Ted Casablanca
- Lee Grant as Miriam Polar
- Naomi Stevens as Miss Steinberg
- Robert H. Harris as Henry Bellamy
- Jacqueline Susann as Reporter #1 at Jennifer's suicide
- Robert Viharo as Art Film Director
- Joey Bishop as Telethon Emcee
- George Jessel - Grammy Awards Emcee
- Richard Dreyfuss - assistant stage manager (uncredited)

Production

- Judy Garland was originally cast as Helen Lawson, but was fired when she showed up to work drunk; Susan Hayward replaced her in the role after production had already begun. On July 20, 2009, Patty Duke appeared at the Castro Theater in San Francisco with a benefit screening of the film, and said that director Mark Robson made Garland wait from 8am to 4pm before filming her scenes for the day, knowing that Garland would be upset and drunk by that time.
- Barbara Parkins suggested Dionne Warwick perform the film's theme song. A re-recorded version of the song became Warwick's biggest hit to date, peaking at the #2 spot in February, 1968.
- Barbara Harris and Petula Clark were seriously considered for the role of Neely O'Hara; Barbara Parkins also tested for the role, although it ultimately went to Patty Duke.
- Thelma Pelish, who appeared as Mae in the movie The Pajama Game, has a bit part in the film as a desk manager at a rehearsal hall.
- Soap opera actress Darlene Conley, who played Sally Spectra on The Bold And The Beautiful, has an uncredited part as a nurse in a sanitarium.
- Judith Lowry, who later appeared in the series *Phyllis* as Phyllis Lindstrom's nemesis, Sally Dexter, played Anne's Aunt Amy, although she wasn't credited.
- The book's author, Jacqueline Susann, appeared in the film as a reporter at the scene of Jennifer's suicide.

- The film's "happy ending" was cobbled together by studio demands for an uplifting dénouement; it strays from the original plot of the book, in which Anne stays with Lyon after his affair with Neely and becomes increasingly dependent on drugs. Writer Harlan Ellison, who wrote the original screenplay, took his name off the project because of the ending and the watering-down of his realistic adaptation of the story.
- *Beyond the Valley of the Dolls*, a 1970 satirical pastiche, was filmed by Twentieth Century-Fox while the studio was being sued by Jacqueline Susann, according to Irving Mansfield's book *Jackie and Me*. Susann created the title for a Jean Holloway-scripted sequel that was rejected by the studio, which allowed Russ Meyer to film a radically different movie with the same title. The suit went to court after Susann's death in 1974; the estate would eventually win damages in the amount of $2 million against Fox.
- This was Richard Dreyfuss' first (uncredited) film appearance.
- Also uncredited, actress Peggy Rea, who later appeared in *The Waltons*, *Step by Step* and *Grace Under Fire* appears briefly as Neely O'Hara's vocal coach.
- Lee Grant has stated in an interview that this was the "Best and funniest worst movie ever made!".

Award nominations
- Academy Award for Best Music, Scoring of Music, Adaptation or Treatment (John Williams)
- Golden Globe Award for Most Promising Newcomer – Female (Sharon Tate)
- Grammy Award for Best Original Score Written for a Motion Picture (André Previn)

Differences between the book and film
- In the film, Anne finds it difficult to leave the beautiful house in Lawrenceville. In the book she despises the cold, austere house and loses Lyon the first time because she refuses to live there with him.
- In the film, Neely O'Hara is cast out of Lawson's new Broadway play. In the book, O'Hara replaces Terry King because Helen prefers that an unknown play the second-lead *ingenue* role, rather than King, who was getting too much attention in the press.
- The film completely excludes the lengthy subplot in which Anne is unwillingly engaged to wealthy but unattractive Alan Cooper while struggling to hide her feelings for Lyon Burke.
- In the book, the story takes place over multiple decades, dealing with the aging of women in Hollywood. The film takes place in a much shorter time span.
- In the book Anne ends up marrying Lyon Burke, who eventually has a serious affair with Neely. Anne does not have the peaceful catharsis in the book that she does in the film; instead she slips into the same drug-induced comatose life that plagued the rest of her friends, while settling for her loveless marriage and her husband's infidelity.

- Like many other characters, George Bellows and Terry King are eliminated completely, though Bellows is mentioned in the beginning of the film by Miss Steinberg.
- In the book the girls share a house and a close friendship. This was totally ignored in the film.
- In the book Anne is blonde; she's a brunette in the film.
- In the book, Helen and Anne become friends because she sees her as someone important since she's engaged to millionaire Alan Cooper.
- In the book, Anne and Neely are very close. Anne had met Neely when she rented a room at the house where Neely is also renting. In the film, Anne rents a hotel room when she first arrives in New York.
- In the book, Neely begs Anne to ask her boss to pull strings to get her a part in the play 'Hit the Sky'; the understudy role she gets begins her career. In the film, Neely leaves the play.
- In the book, Anne does not feel passionate about any men—not her Lawrenceville beau, not Alan Cooper, not Mr. Gilmore—only Lyon. The film only depicts that she falls for Lyon.
- In the book Jennifer North was in the midst of a divorce with a European prince when she first appears. This is not mentioned in the film.
- In the book Jenn is engaged to a politician with whom she's deeply in love by the time she's diagnosed with breast cancer. This is completely exclude in the movie, which claims that North is in love with Tony Polar until the end of her life.

Soundtrack

Valley of the Dolls (Soundtrack)	
Studio album by Various	
Released	1967
Recorded	1967
Genre	Pop, Romantic Ballad
Label	20th Century Fox Records

The soundtrack was released in 1967. Dionne Warwick sang the title track on the film; however, her version is not on the soundtrack. Warwick was signed to Scepter Records at the time and could not contractually appear. Therefore, a re-recorded version appears on the LP *Dionne Warwick in Valley of the Dolls*.

Margaret Whiting recorded "I'll Plant My Own Tree" for the film, while Eileen Wilson recorded it for the soundtrack album: the song is dubbed for Susan Hayward, while "It's Impossible" and "Give a Little More" are both dubbed by Gail Heideman for Patty Duke. Both Heideman and Wilson are uncredited on the soundtrack label.

Track listing

1. Theme From "Valley Of The Dolls (04:04) Vocal: Dory Previn - Narration By Barbara Parkins
2. It's Impossible (02:12) Vocal: Gail Heideman (for Patty Duke)
3. Ann At Lawrenceville (02:37) Instrumental
4. Chance Meeting (02:31) Instrumental
5. Neely's Career Montage (01:59) Instrumental
6. Come Live With Me (02:01) Vocal: Tony Scotti
7. I'll Plant My Own Tree (02:24) Vocal: Eileen Wilson (for Susan Hayward) Margaret Whiting dubbed Susan Hayward in the film but she was under contract to a different label, so veteran voice double Eileen Wilson sings "I'll Plant My Own Tree" on the soundtrack album.
8. The Gillian Girl Commercial (02:04) Instrumental
9. Jennifer's French Movie (02:26) Instrumental
10. Give A Little More (02:02) Vocal: Gail Heideman (for Patty Duke)
11. Jennifer's Recollection (02:52) Instrumental (contain a reprise of Come Live With Me vocal: by Tony Scotti)
12. Theme From "Valley Of The Dolls Reprise (03:00) Vocal: Dory Previn

The original version of "I'll Plant My Own Tree", as recorded by Judy Garland before she was fired from the film production, was finally released in 1976 on an obscure compilation LP entitled *Cut! Out-takes from Hollywood's Greatest Musicals*.

External links

- *Valley of the Dolls* [1] at the Internet Movie Database
- *Valley of the Dolls* [2] at Allmovie
- *Valley of the Dolls* [3] at Rotten Tomatoes

Rosemary's Baby (film)

Rosemary's Baby	
Theatrical release poster	
Directed by	Roman Polanski
Produced by	William Castle
Written by	Roman Polanski **Novel:** Ira Levin
Starring	Mia Farrow John Cassavetes Ruth Gordon Sidney Blackmer Maurice Evans Ralph Bellamy
Music by	Krzysztof Komeda
Cinematography	William A. Fraker
Editing by	Sam O'Steen Bob Wyman
Distributed by	Paramount Pictures
Release date(s)	June 12, 1968
Running time	136 minutes
Country	United States
Language	English
Budget	$2.3 million
Gross revenue	$33,395,426
Followed by	*Look What's Happened to Rosemary's Baby*

Rosemary's Baby is a 1968 American horror film written and directed by Roman Polanski, based on the bestselling 1967 novel by Ira Levin. The cast includes Mia Farrow, John Cassavetes, Ruth Gordon, Maurice Evans, Sidney Blackmer, and Charles Grodin. The film received mostly positive reviews and earned numerous nominations and awards. The American Film Institute ranked the film 9th in their *100 Years...100 Thrills* list. The official tagline of the film is "Pray for Rosemary's Baby."

Plot summary

Rosemary Woodhouse (Mia Farrow), a bright but somewhat naive young housewife, and Guy (John Cassavetes), her husband and a struggling actor, move into the Bramford, a Gothic, 19th century New York City apartment building with a history of unsavory tenants and mysterious events. Their neighbors are an elderly and slightly eccentric couple, Minnie and Roman Castevet (Ruth Gordon and Sidney Blackmer), who tend to be meddlesome but seem harmless. Guy becomes unusually close to the pair while Rosemary tries to maintain a distance from them. Guy lands a role in a play when the actor originally cast suddenly and inexplicably goes blind. Soon afterward, Guy suggests that he and Rosemary have the child they had planned. On the night they plan to try to conceive, Minnie brings them individual ramekins of chocolate mousse, but Rosemary finds hers has a chalky under-taste and surreptitiously throws it away after a few mouthfuls. Shortly afterward, she has a dizzy spell and passes out. She experiences what she perceives to be a strange dream in which she is raped by a demonic presence.

A few weeks later, Rosemary learns she is pregnant and is due on June 28, 1966 (6/66). She plans to receive obstetric care from Dr. Hill, recommended by her friend Elise (Emmaline Henry), but the Castevets insist she see their good friend, famed obstetrician, Dr. Sapirstein (Ralph Bellamy). For the first three months of her pregnancy, Rosemary suffers severe abdominal pains, loses weight, and craves raw meat and chicken liver. The doctor insists the pain will subside soon and assures her she has nothing to worry about. At the Castavets' New Year's Eve party, Roman raises a toast to "1966: the Year One".

When her old friend Hutch sees Rosemary's gaunt appearance, he is disturbed enough to do some research, and plans to share his findings with her but falls into a coma before they can meet. He briefly regains consciousness before he dies, and instructs his friend Grace Cardiff to deliver the book about witchcraft on his desk that he had planned to give to Rosemary. Photographs, passages in the text he marked, and the cryptic message "the name is an anagram" lead Rosemary to realize Roman Castevet is really Steven Marcato, the son of Adrian Marcato, a former resident of the Bramford who was accused of worshiping Satan and was a martyr to the cause. She suspects her neighbors are part of a cult with sinister designs for her baby, and Guy is cooperating with them in exchange for their help in advancing his career. She deduces that Dr. Saperstein is also part of the conspiracy when his receptionist comments that the smell coming from a good luck charm given to Rosemary by the Castavets — which contains tannis root, also known as "Devil's Pepper" — reminds her of a fragrance often shared by the doctor.

An increasingly disturbed Rosemary shares her fears and suspicions with Dr. Hill, who, assuming she is delusional, calls Dr. Sapirstein and Guy. She is told that if she cooperates, she and the baby will not be harmed. The two men bring Rosemary home, at which point she goes into labor. When she awakens following the delivery of her baby, she is told the child died shortly after birth. However, when she hears an infant's cries somewhere in the building, she suspects he still is alive. In the hall closet, she discovers a secret door leading into the Castevet apartment where the coven meets, and finds the congregation gathered, worshipping her newborn son, the spawn of Satan. The truth is revealed about Rosemary's son being the Antichrist, devastating Rosemary considerably. Both Roman and the coven urge Rosemary to become a mother to her son, Adrian. The film ends with her adjusting her son's blankets and gently rocking his cradle.

Cast

- Mia Farrow as Rosemary Woodhouse
- John Cassavetes as Guy Woodhouse
- Ruth Gordon as Minnie Castevet
- Sidney Blackmer as Roman Castevet / Steven Marcato
- Maurice Evans as Hutch
- Ralph Bellamy as Dr. Abraham Sapirstein
- Charles Grodin as Dr. Hill
- Patsy Kelly as Laura-Louise
- Victoria Vetri as Terry Gionoffrio
- Emmaline Henry as Elise Dunstan
- Hanna Landy as Grace Cardiff
- Tony Curtis as voice of Donald Baumgart

Production

Script

In *Rosemary's Baby: A Retrospective*, a featurette on the DVD release of the film, screenwriter/director Roman Polanski, Paramount Pictures executive Robert Evans, and production designer Richard Sylbert reminisce at length about the production. Evans recalled William Castle brought him the galley proofs of the book and asked him to purchase the film rights even before Random House released the publication. The studio head recognized the commercial potential of the project and agreed with the stipulation that Castle, who had a reputation for low-budget horror films, could produce but not direct the film adaptation. He makes a cameo as the man at the phone booth waiting for Mia Farrow to finish her call.

Evans admired Polanski's European films and hoped he could convince him to make his American debut with *Rosemary's Baby*. He knew the director was a ski buff who was anxious to make a film with the sport as its basis, so he sent him the script for *Downhill Racer* along with the galleys for *Rosemary*. Polanski read the latter book non-stop through the night and called Evans the following morning to tell him he thought *Rosemary* was the more interesting project, and would like the opportunity to write as well as direct it.

Polanski, having never before adapted a screenplay, was not aware that he was allowed to make changes from the source material, leading to the film being extremely faithful to the novel and including many lines of dialogue drawn directly from Levin's book. Author Ira Levin claimed that during a scene in which Guy mentions wanting to buy a particular shirt advertised in *The New Yorker*, Polanski was unable to find the specific issue with the shirt advertised and phoned Levin for help. Levin, who had assumed while writing that any given issue of *The New Yorker* would contain an ad for men's shirts, admitted that he had made it up.

Casting

Polanski envisioned Rosemary as a robust, full-figured, girl-next-door type, and he wanted Tuesday Weld or his own wife Sharon Tate for the role. Since the book had not reached bestseller status yet, Evans was unsure the title alone would guarantee an audience for the film, and he felt a bigger name was needed for the lead. Patty Duke was considered for the lead. With only a supporting role in *Guns at Batasi* (1964) and the not-yet-released *A Dandy in Aspic* (1968) as her only feature film credits, Mia Farrow had an unproven box office track record, but her role as Allison MacKenzie in the popular television series *Peyton Place* and her unexpected marriage to Frank Sinatra had made her a household name. Despite her waif-like appearance (which would ultimately prove beneficial to the character, as Rosemary became more frail as her pregnancy progressed), Polanski agreed to cast her. Her acceptance incensed Sinatra, who had demanded she forgo her career when they wed, and he served her divorce papers via a corporate lawyer, in front of the cast and crew midway through filming. In an effort to salvage her relationship, Farrow asked Evans to release her from her contract, but he persuaded her to remain with the project after showing her an hour-long rough cut and assuring her she would receive an Academy Award nomination for her performance.

Robert Redford was the first choice for the role of Guy Woodhouse, but he turned down the offer. Jack Nicholson was considered briefly before Polanski suggested John Cassavetes.

Sylbert was a good friend of Garson Kanin, who was married to Ruth Gordon, and he suggested her for the role of Minnie Castevet. He also suggested The Dakota, an Upper West Side apartment building known for its show business tenants, be used for the Bramford. Its hallways were not as worn and dark as Polanski wanted, but when the building's owners would not allow interior filming, that became a moot point and it was used for exterior shots only.

Polanski wanted to cast Hollywood old-timers as the coven members but did not know any by name. He drew sketches of how he envisioned each character, and they were used to fill the roles. In every instance, the actor cast strongly resembled Polanski's drawing. These included Ralph Bellamy, Patsy Kelly, Elisha Cook, Jr., Phil Leeds, and Hope Summers.

When Rosemary calls Donald Baumgart, the actor who goes blind and is replaced by Guy, the voice heard is that of actor Tony Curtis. Farrow, who had not been told who would be reading Baumgart's lines, recognized the voice but could not place it. The slight confusion she displays throughout the call was exactly what Polanski hoped to capture by not revealing Curtis' identity in advance.

Filming

Sydney Guilaroff designed the wig worn by Mia Farrow in the film's early scenes. It was removed to reveal the Vidal Sassoon hairdo that made headlines when Farrow cut her trademark long hair during filming of *Peyton Place*.

One of Mia Farrow's more emotionally charged scenes occurs in the midst of a party, when several of Rosemary's female friends lock Guy out of the kitchen as they console her in private. The scene was shot in a single day. That morning, just before the first take was filmed, a private messenger served Farrow with formal divorce papers from Frank Sinatra. As she read the documents, Farrow fell to her knees on the kitchen floor and openly wept in front of the cast and crew. Roman Polanski insisted that the day be canceled and filming be postponed until the next day, when he would start consecutively filming as many scenes as possible that did not contain Rosemary. Farrow openly would not accept this, insisting that nothing had changed. The day's filming concluded on time and without delay.

When Farrow was reluctant to film a scene that depicted a dazed and preoccupied Rosemary wandering into the middle of a Manhattan street into oncoming traffic, Polanski pointed to her pregnancy padding and reassured her, "no one's going to hit a pregnant woman". The scene was successfully shot with Farrow walking into real traffic and Polanski following along, operating the hand-held camera since he was the only one willing to do it.

Critical reception

In her review for *The New York Times*, Renata Adler said, "The movie—although it is pleasant—doesn't seem to work on any of its dark or powerful terms. I think this is because it is almost too extremely plausible. The quality of the young people's lives seems the quality of lives that one knows, even to the point of finding old people next door to avoid and lean on. One gets very annoyed that they don't catch on sooner."

Roger Ebert of the *Chicago Sun-Times* called it "a brooding, macabre film, filled with the sense of unthinkable danger. Strangely enough it also has an eerie sense of humor almost until the end. It is a creepy film and a crawly film, and a film filled with things that go bump in the night. It is very good...much more than just a suspense story; the brilliance of the film comes more from Polanski's direction, and from a series of genuinely inspired performances, than from the original story . . . The best thing that can be said about the film, I think, is that it works. Polanski has taken a most difficult situation and made it believable, right up to the end. In this sense, he even outdoes Hitchcock."

Variety stated, "Several exhilarating milestones are achieved in *Rosemary's Baby*, an excellent film version of Ira Levin's diabolical chiller novel. Writer-director Roman Polanski has triumphed in his first US-made pic. The film holds attention without explicit violence or gore . . . Farrow's performance is outstanding."

Today, the film is widely regarded as a classic; 53 of the 54 reviews surveyed on the review aggregator website Rotten Tomatoes are positive.

Legacy

In the 1976 television film, *Look What's Happened to Rosemary's Baby*, Patty Duke starred as Rosemary Woodhouse and Ruth Gordon reprised her role of Minnie Castevet.

For the scene where Rosemary is raped by Satan, *Rosemary's Baby* ranked #23 on Bravo's *100 Scariest Movie Moments*. Contrary to an urban legend, Anton LaVey did not play the role of Satan in the rape scene of *Rosemary's Baby*. In fact it was actor Clay Tanner, and no technical advisor was used.

Thirty years after he wrote *Rosemary's Baby*, Ira Levin wrote *Son of Rosemary*, a sequel which he dedicated to the film's star, Mia Farrow. Reaction to the book was mixed, but it made the best seller lists nationwide.

A 2009-2010 remake of *Rosemary's Baby* was briefly considered. The intended producers were Michael Bay, Andrew Form, and Brad Fuller. The remake fell through in 2008.

Awards and honors

Academy Awards

- Academy Award for Best Supporting Actress (Ruth Gordon, **winner**)
- Academy Award for Best Adapted Screenplay (nominee)

Golden Globe Awards

- Golden Globe Award for Best Supporting Actress - Motion Picture (Gordon, **winner**)
- Golden Globe Award for Best Actress - Motion Picture Drama (Farrow, nominee)
- Golden Globe Award for Best Screenplay (nominee)
- Golden Globe Award for Best Original Score (nominee)

Other awards

- BAFTA Award for Best Actress in a Leading Role (Mia Farrow, nominee)
- Directors Guild of America Award for Outstanding Directorial Achievement in Motion Pictures (nominee)
- Writers Guild of America Award for Best Written American Drama (nominee)
- David di Donatello Award for Best Foreign Actress (Mia Farrow, **winner**)
- David di Donatello Award for Best Foreign Director (**winner**)
- Edgar Allan Poe Award for Best Motion Picture Screenplay (nominee)
- French Syndicate of Cinema Critics Award for Best Foreign Film (**winner**)
- Kansas City Film Critics Circle Award for Best Supporting Actor (Sidney Blackmer, **winner**)

- Kansas City Film Critics Circle Award for Best Supporting Actress (Gordon, **winner**)

In popular culture

The film has been parodied in numerous works since its 1968 release, including *Mad Magazine* ("Rosemia's Boo-Boo", issue #124, January 1969) and *The Realist* ("Rosemerica's Baby", No. 93, August 1972).

References to the film can also be found in innumerable music and television works. Some artists who have featured references to the film within their music include Interpol, Microfilm (band), Charles Bronson, The Devil Wears Prada, The Tubes, Today Is the Day, Walt Mink and Fantômas. The hardcore punk band Rosemary's Babies took the pluralized version of the title as a statement of their horror film influences. The film has also been referenced in several television shows and other films, including *That '70s Show, Bébé's Kids, South Park, Star Trek: Enterprise, Chapter 27, Stay Tuned, Last Action Hero, Ugly Americans, Frasier, Weeds, Angels in America*, CSI, Gilmore Girls and *Roseanne*.

Following the film's premier, a string of movies about Satan worshippers and black magic appeared on the low budget-big budget scene. Among those films made and released were *The Devil Rides Out, The Brotherhood Of Satan, Mark Of The Devil* and *Blood On Satan's Claw*. They offered up new views of good against evil, especially when Devil worship caused concern in the modern world.

External links

- *Rosemary's Baby* [1] at the Internet Movie Database
- *Rosemary's Baby* [2] at the TCM Movie Database
- *Rosemary's Baby* [3] at Allmovie
- *Rosemary's Baby* [4] at Rotten Tomatoes
- Dialogue Transcript at Script-o-rama.com [5]
- William Castle's involvement in the film [6]

The Wrecking Crew (1969 film)

The Wrecking Crew	
original film poster by Robert McGinnis	
Directed by	Phil Karlson
Produced by	Irving Allen
Written by	William P. McGivern
Starring	Dean Martin Elke Sommer Sharon Tate Nancy Kwan
Music by	Hugo Montenegro
Cinematography	Sam Leavitt
Editing by	Maury Winetrobe
Distributed by	Columbia Pictures
Release date(s)	1969
Running time	105 minutes
Preceded by	The Ambushers

The Wrecking Crew, released in 1968 and starring Dean Martin, Elke Sommer and Sharon Tate is the fourth and final film in a series of American comedy-spy-fi theatrical releases featuring Martin as secret agent Matt Helm. As with the previous three movies (*The Silencers*, *Murderers' Row* and *The Ambushers*), the film is based only loosely upon Donald Hamilton's 1960 novel of the same title and takes great liberties with the plot and characters, being developed as a spoof of the James Bond films. *The Wrecking Crew* was the second Helm novel published and the earliest of the books to be adapted.

In a plotline reminiscent of the Bond novel/film, *Goldfinger*, Helm is assigned by his secret agency, ICE, to bring down an evil count who is trying to collapse the world economy by stealing gold. Along the way, Helm is reluctantly partnered with a British agent played by Sharon Tate (in one of her final appearances on film before her murder at the hands of Charles Manson's followers.) Chuck Norris makes his film debut in a small role, and Bruce Lee is credited with being the film's karate advisor.

Also appearing in the film are Nancy Kwan as Yu-Rang, Tina Louise as Lola Medina, and Nigel Green as the villainous Count Contini. Macdonald, Helm's chief, is played by John Larch in this film, replacing James Gregory, who played the role in the other three films. Gregory said in an interview in *Filmfax* magazine that he was sent a reduced amount for his fee in the film. He was told that the film was reducing its budget but Gregory refused to take the lower fee. This is also the only film in the series not to feature Helm's secretary, Lovesy Kravesit played by Beverly Adams.

Music

Hugo Montenegro composed the score for the film, and Mack David and Frank DeVol wrote the theme song played over the opening and end credits, "House of Seven Joys" that was the working title of the film.

Reception

Critical response to this film varies, with some calling it the worst of the series, where it mostly features Helm playing up to glamorous women and the storyline is the bits that join those many encounters together. There was also some poor acting and the film had many minor mistakes in it which should have been edited out as well as so-so special effects. Others called it the best due to its reduced reliance on outlandish gadgets and story lines. It was the first film in the series to not be written by comedy writer Herbert Baker but by former police reporter and crime novel author William P. McGivern. It is also notable for the appearance of Tate and martial arts scenes cheroeographed by Bruce Lee.

Legacy

The film ends with the announcement of a fifth Matt Helm film, *The Ravagers* (which would have been based upon Hamilton's 1964 novel of the same title). However, Dean Martin declined to return for another film in the face of a declining box office. When Martin refused to make *The Ravagers*, Columbia held up Martin's share of the profits on *Murderers' Row*. The project was then cancelled.

A "Tony Rome Meets Matt Helm" movie with Frank Sinatra reprising the character he had played in the films *Tony Rome* (1967) and *Lady in Cement* was also bandied about, but never amounted to anything.

Several years later, a *Matt Helm* TV series featuring Tony Franciosa would be attempted, but in a much more serious vein, and it was unsuccessful. As of 2009, early planning for a new Matt Helm-based film was underway through DreamWorks.

Cast

- Dean Martin as Matt Helm
- Elke Sommer as Linka Karensky
- Sharon Tate as Freya Carlson
- Nancy Kwan as Yu-Rang
- Nigel Green as Count Contini
- Tina Louise as Lola Medina
- John Larch as 'Mac' MacDonald
- John Brascia as Karl
- Weaver Levy as Kim
- Wilhelm von Homburg as Gregor
- Bill Saito as Ching
- Fuji as Toki
- Pepper Martin as Frankie
- Ted H. Jordan as Guard
- Whitney Chase as Miss Natural Gas (uncredited)
- David Chow as Bartender (uncredited)
- Noel Drayton as Man at Downing Street Meeting (uncredited)
- Tony Giorgio as Gadget Agent for I.C.E. (uncredited)
- Joséphine James as Girl (uncredited)
- Kenner G. Kemp as Officer in Hospital Room (uncredited)
- John Kowal as Kelly (uncredited)
- James Lloyd as Desk Clerk (uncredited)
- Byron Morrow as Officer in Hospital Room (uncredited)
- Chuck Norris as Man in the House of 7 Joys (uncredited)
  - This movie was Chuck Norris' film debut.
- Allen Pinson as Page (uncredited)
- Bartlett Robinson as President's Aide (uncredited)
- Bill M. Ryusaki as Henri (uncredited)
- Dick Winslow as Man (uncredited)

Uncredited
- James Daris
- Harry Fleer
- Harry Geldard
- Joe Gray
- Rex Holman
- Brick Huston
- J. B. Pick
- Vincent Van Lynn

Miscellaneous credits: Bruce Lee as choreographer for the fight scenes. World Karate and Kickboxing Champion Joe Lewis and American Kenpo Founder Ed Parker both had fight scenes with Dean Martin.

External links
- *The Wrecking Crew* [1] at the Internet Movie Database

The Thirteen Chairs

The Thirteen Chairs	
1986 Force Video VHS cover	
Directed by	Nicolas Gessner Luciano Lucignani
Produced by	Claude Giroux Edward J. Pope
Written by	Antonio Altoviti Marc Behm Nicolas Gessner
Starring	Vittorio Gassman Sharon Tate Orson Welles
Music by	Stelvio Cipriani Carlo Rustichelli
Cinematography	Giuseppe Ruzzolini
Studio	C.E.F. (Rome) and C.O.F.C.I. (Paris)
Distributed by	Avco Embassy
Release date(s)	**Italy** (as *12 + 1*): October 7, 1969 **United States** (as *The Thirteen Chairs*): May 1, 1970
Running time	94 min.
Language	English

The Thirteen Chairs (Original title: *12 + 1*) is a comedy film released in 1969. It was based on *The Twelve Chairs*, a 1928 satirical novel by the Soviet authors Ilf and Petrov. It was directed by Nicolas Gessner and Luciano Lucignani, and starred Sharon Tate (her last film before her murder), Vittorio Gassman, Orson Welles, Vittorio De Sica and Tim Brooke-Taylor. Most of it was filmed in Italy.

Synopsis

Mario Beretti (Vittorio Gassman) is an Italian-American and a young philanderer, who has migrated to New York City. He is also a Barber. He runs a Barber Shop by a construction site that boasts few customers. His life reaches a turning point when he is notified of the death of his aunt living in England, who named him her sole heir.

Mario rushes to England, and learns that his inheritance consists of thirteen antique chairs. He sells them in order to cover his transportation costs, but soon learns from his aunt's last message, that inside one of the chairs is a fortune in jewels.

He tries to buy back the chairs but is unsuccessful in doing so. With the help of a lovely antique dealer living in London named Pat (Sharon Tate), the two then set out on a bizarre quest to track down the chairs that takes them from London to Rome. Along the way, they meet a bunch of equally bizarre characters such as a driver of a furniture moving van named Albert (Terry-Thomas), a prostitute named Judy (Mylène Demongeot), the leader of a traveling theater company that stages a poor version of *Dr. Jekyll and Mr. Hyde* (Orson Welles), the Italian entrepreneur Carlo Di Seta (Vittorio De Sica), and his vivacious daughter Stefanella (Ottavia Piccolo).

The bizarre chase ends in Rome, where the chair containing the money finds its way into a truck, and is collected by nuns who auction it off to charity. With nothing much left to do as a result of the failure in his quest, Mario travels back to New York City by ship, as Pat sees him off and waves goodbye to him.

The film ends with Mario returning to New York City, and to his Barber Shop. His friends over at the other (and more lavish) shop join him, as do two construction workers, and his last customer Randomhouse (Lionel Jeffries). It is there that Mario makes an strange discovery: Shortly before his departure for Europe, he invented a way to make hair regrow miraculously. He then laughs evilly over his discovery.

Trivia

- Filmed from February–April 1969. [1]
- Because the script for Sharon Tate's scenes called for several semi-nude scenes, the director arranged to film those scenes first. As filming (and her pregnancy) progressed, the director obscured Tate's stomach with large purses and scarves. This is most apparent in the scene following her ride in the furniture mover's van.
- In response to her recent murder, Sharon Tate received top billing for this film (this film was released posthumously). In addition, several of her other films (including *Valley of the Dolls*) were reissued to give her top billing on the theater marquees.
- This film is extremely hard to find on VHS. It was released through rental only by Force Video in 1986 under the *Thirteen Chairs* name, and again a year later by Continental Video, under the original *12 + 1* name. On March 12, 2008, the film was released on DVD in Italy by 01 Distribution.

This version is in Italian, lacks English subtitles, and doesn't include an English audio track.

Cast
- Sharon Tate as Pat
- Vittorio Gassman as Mario Beretti
- Orson Welles as Maurice Markau
- Vittorio De Sica as Carlo Di Seta - The Commendatore
- Terry-Thomas as Albert
- Mylène Demongeot as Judy
- Grégoire Aslan as Psychiatrist
- Tim Brooke-Taylor as Jackie
- John Steiner as Stanley Duncan
- William Rushton as Lionel Bennett
- Michele Borelli as Rosy
- Lionel Jeffries as Randomhouse
- Ottavia Piccolo as Stefanella Di Seta
- Catana Cayetano as Véronique
- Claude Berthy as François
- Marzio Margine as Pasqualino
- Alfred Thomas as Mbama
- Antonio Altoviti as Mr. Greenwood

Uncredited
- Marc Fiorini as Maurizio Fiorini
- Edda Albertini
- Luigi Bonos
- Alfredo Colzi
- Sandro Dori
- Tom Felleghy
- Piero Gerlini
- Fiona Lewis as 'Angel Antiques' Salesperson
- Joe Martinelli
- Corrado Olmi
- Mirella Pamphili
- Mimmo Poli

External links

- *The Thirteen Chairs* [2] at the Internet Movie Database

Famous Co-stars

Julie Andrews

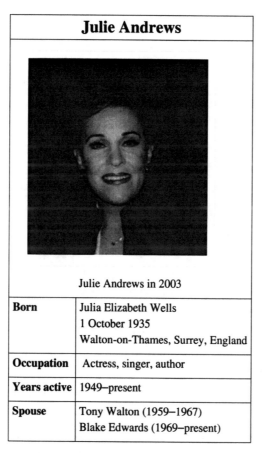

Julie Andrews	
Born	Julia Elizabeth Wells 1 October 1935 Walton-on-Thames, Surrey, England
Occupation	Actress, singer, author
Years active	1949–present
Spouse	Tony Walton (1959–1967) Blake Edwards (1969–present)

Julie Andrews in 2003

Dame **Julia Elizabeth Andrews**, DBE (*née* **Wells**; born 1 October 1935) is an English film and stage actress, singer, and author. She is the recipient of Golden Globe, Emmy, Grammy, BAFTA, People's Choice Award, Theatre World Award, Screen Actors Guild and Academy Award honours. Andrews was a former British child actress and singer who made her Broadway debut in 1954 with *The Boy Friend*, and rose to prominence starring in other musicals such as *My Fair Lady* and *Camelot*, and in musical films such as *Mary Poppins* (1964), for which she won the Academy Award for Best Actress, and *The Sound of Music* (1965): the roles for which she is still best-known. Her voice spanned four octaves until it was damaged by a throat operation in 1997.

Andrews had a major revival of her film career in 2000s in family films such as *The Princess Diaries* (2001), its sequel *The Princess Diaries 2: Royal Engagement* (2004), and the *Shrek* animated films (2004–2010). In 2003 Andrews revisited her first Broadway success, this time as a stage director, with a revival of *The Boy Friend* at the Bay Street Theatre, Sag Harbor, New York (and later at the Goodspeed Opera House, in East Haddam, Connecticut in 2005).

Andrews is also an author of children's books, and in 2008 published an autobiography, *Home: A Memoir of My Early Years*.

Early life

Julie Andrews was born **Julia Elizabeth Wells** on 1 October 1935 in Walton-on-Thames, Surrey, England. Her mother, Barbara Wells (née Morris), was married to Edward C. "Ted" Wells, a teacher of metal and woodworking, but Andrews was conceived as a result of an affair her mother had with a family friend.

With the outbreak of World War II, Barbara and Ted Wells went their separate ways. Ted Wells assisted with evacuating children to Surrey during the Blitz, while Barbara joined Ted Andrews in entertaining the troops through the good offices of the Entertainments National Service Association (ENSA). Barbara and Ted Wells were soon divorced. They both remarried: Barbara to Ted Andrews, in 1939; and Ted Wells, to a former hairstylist working a lathe at a war factory that employed them both in Hinchley Wood, Surrey.

Julia Wells lived briefly with Ted Wells and her brother John in Surrey. In about 1940, Ted Wells sent Julia to live with her mother and stepfather, who, the elder Wells thought, would be better able to provide for his talented daughter's artistic training. According to her 2008 autobiography *Home*, while Julia had been used to calling Ted Andrews "Uncle Ted", her mother suggested it would be more appropriate to refer to her stepfather as "Pop", while her father remained "Dad" or "Daddy" to her. Julia disliked this change.

The Andrews family was "very poor and we lived in a bad slum area of London," Andrews recalled, adding, "That was a very black period in my life." In addition, according to Andrews's 2008 memoir, her stepfather was an alcoholic. Ted Andrews twice, while drunk, tried to get into bed with his stepdaughter, resulting in Andrews putting a lock on her door. But, as the stage career of Ted and Barbara Andrews improved, they were able to afford to move to better surroundings, first to Beckenham and then, as the war ended, back to the Andrews's home town of Walton-on-Thames. The Andrews family took up residence at The Old Meuse, a house where Andrews's maternal grandmother happened to have served as a maid.

Julie Andrews' stepfather sponsored lessons for her, first at the Cone-Ripman School, an independent arts educational school in London, then with the famous concert soprano and voice instructor Lilian Stiles-Allen. "She had an enormous influence on me", Andrews said of Stiles-Allen, adding, "She was my third mother – I've got more mothers and fathers than anyone in the world." In her 2008 autobiography *Home*, Andrews denies having perfect pitch. After Cone-Ripman School, Andrews continued her academic education at the nearby Woodbrook School, a local state school in Beckenham.

Early career in UK

Julie Andrews performed spontaneously and unbilled on stage with her parents for about two years beginning in 1945. "Then came the day when I was told I must go to bed in the afternoon because I was going to be allowed to sing with Mummy and Pop in the evening," Andrews explained. She would stand on a beer crate to reach the microphone and sing, sometimes a solo or as a duet with her stepfather, while her mother played piano. "It must have been ghastly, but it seemed to go down all right."

Julie Andrews got her big break when her stepfather introduced her to Val Parnell, whose Moss Empires controlled prominent venues in London. Andrews made her professional solo debut at the London Hippodrome singing the difficult aria "Je Suis Titania" from *Mignon* as part of a musical revue called "Starlight Roof" on 22 October 1947. She played the Hippodrome for one year. Andrews recalled "Starlight Roof" saying, "There was this wonderful American entertainer and comedian, Wally Boag, who made balloon animals. He would say, 'Is there any little girl or boy in the audience who would like one of these?' And I would rush up onstage and say, 'I'd like one, please.' And then he would chat to me and I'd tell him I sang... I was fortunate in that I absolutely stopped the show cold. I mean, the audience went crazy."

On 1 November 1948, Julie Andrews became the youngest solo performer ever to be seen in a Royal Command Variety Performance, at the London Palladium, where she performed along with Danny Kaye, the Nicholas Brothers and the comedy team George and Bert Bernard for members of King George VI's family.

Julie Andrews followed her parents into radio and television. She reportedly made her television debut on the BBC program *RadiOlympia Showtime* on 8 October 1949. She garnered considerable fame throughout the United Kingdom for her work on the BBC radio comedy show *Educating Archie*; she was a cast member from 1950 to 1952.

Andrews appeared on West End Theatre at the London Casino, where she played one year each as Princess Badroulbadour in *Aladdin* and the egg in *Humpty Dumpty*. She also appeared on provincial stages across United Kingdom in *Jack and the Beanstalk* and *Little Red Riding Hood*, as well as starring as the lead role in *Cinderella*.

In 1950 at the age of 14, Andrews was asked to sing at a party of a family friend, Katherine Norwalk, and it was then that she learned that Ted Wells was not her biological father.

Early career in the U.S.

On 30 September 1954 on the eve of her 19th birthday, Julie Andrews made her Broadway debut portraying "Polly Browne" in the already highly successful London musical *The Boy Friend*. To the critics, Andrews was the stand-out performer in the show. Near the end of her *Boy Friend* contract, Andrews was asked to audition for *My Fair Lady* on Broadway and got the part. In November 1955 Andrews was signed to appear with Bing Crosby in what is regarded as the first made-for-television movie, *High Tor*.

Andrews auditioned for a part in the Richard Rodgers musical *Pipe Dream*. Although Rodgers wanted her for *Pipe Dream*, he advised her to take the part in the Frederick Loewe and Alan Jay Lerner musical *My Fair Lady* if it was offered to her. In 1956, she appeared in *My Fair Lady* as Eliza Doolittle to Rex Harrison's Henry Higgins. Rodgers was so impressed with Andrews's talent that concurrent with her run in *My Fair Lady* she was featured in the Rodgers and Hammerstein television musical, *Cinderella*. *Cinderella* was broadcast live on CBS on 31 March 1957 under the musical direction of Alfredo Antonini and attracted an estimated 107 million viewers.

Miss Andrews married set designer Tony Walton on 10 May 1959 in Weybridge, Surrey. They had first met in 1948 when Andrews was appearing at the London Casino in the show *Humpty Dumpty*. The couple filed for a divorce on November 14, 1967.

Between 1958 and 1962, Andrews appeared on such specials as CBS-TV's *The Fabulous Fifties* and NBC-TV's *The Broadway of Lerner & Loewe*. In addition to guest starring on *The Ed Sullivan Show*, she also appeared on *The Dinah Shore Chevy Show*, *What's My Line?*, *The Jack Benny Program*, *The Bell Telephone Hour*, and *The Garry Moore Show*. In June 1962 Andrews co-starred in *Julie and Carol at Carnegie Hall*, a CBS special with Carol Burnett.

In 1960 Lerner and Loewe again cast her in a period musical as Queen Guinevere in *Camelot*, with Richard Burton and newcomer Robert Goulet. However movie studio head Jack Warner decided Andrews lacked sufficient name recognition for her casting in the film version of *My Fair Lady*; Eliza was played by the established film actress Audrey Hepburn instead. As Warner later recalled, the decision was easy, "In my business I have to know who brings people and their money to a movie theatre box office. Audrey Hepburn had never made a financial flop."

Career peak

Andrews played the title role in Disney's *Mary Poppins*. Walt Disney had seen a performance of *Camelot* and thought Andrews would be perfect for the role of the British nanny who is "practically perfect in every way!" Andrews initially declined because of pregnancy, but Disney politely insisted, saying, "We'll wait for you". Andrews and her husband headed back to the United Kingdom in September 1962 to await the birth of daughter Emma Katherine Walton, who was born in London two months later. The family returned to America in 1963 and Miss Andrews began the film.

As a result of her performance in *Mary Poppins*, Andrews won the 1964 Academy Award for Best Actress and the 1965 Golden Globe Award for Best Actress – Motion Picture Musical or Comedy. She and her *Mary Poppins* co-stars also won the 1965 Grammy Award for Best Album for Children. As a measure of "sweet revenge," as *Poppins* songwriter Richard M. Sherman put it, Andrews closed her acceptance speech at the Golden Globes by saying, "And, finally, my thanks to a man who made a wonderful movie and who made all this possible in the first place, Mr. Jack Warner."

In 1964 she appeared opposite James Garner in *The Americanization of Emily* (1964), which she has described as her favourite film. In 1966, Andrews won her second Golden Globe Award for Best Actress – Motion Picture Musical or Comedy and was nominated for the 1965 Academy Award for Best Actress for her role as Maria von Trapp in *The Sound of Music*.

After completing *The Sound Of Music*, Andrews appeared as a guest star on the NBC-TV variety series *The Andy Williams Show*, which gained her an Emmy nomination. She followed this television appearance with an Emmy Award-winning color special, *The Julie Andrews Show*, which featured Gene Kelly and The New Christy Minstrels as guests. It aired on NBC-TV in November 1965.

In 1966 Andrews starred with Paul Newman in the Hitchcock thriller *Torn Curtain*. By the end of 1967, Andrews had appeared in the television special *Cinderella*; the biggest Broadway musical of its time, *My Fair Lady*; the largest-selling long-playing album, the original cast recording of *My Fair Lady*; the biggest hit in Disney's history, *Mary Poppins*; the highest grossing movie of 1966, *Hawaii*; the biggest and second biggest hits in Universal's history, *Thoroughly Modern Millie* and *Torn Curtain*; and the biggest hit in 20th Century Fox's history *The Sound of Music*.

Mid-career

Andrews, appeared in *Star!*, a 1968 biopic of Gertrude Lawrence, and *Darling Lili* (1970), co-starring Rock Hudson and directed by her soon-to-be second husband, Blake Edwards (they married in 1969). She made only two other films in the 1970s, *The Tamarind Seed* and *10*.

In the 70's, Edwards and Andrews adopted two daughters; Amy in 1974 and Joanna in 1975. Mr. Edwards children from a previous marriage, Jennifer and Geoffrey, were 3 and 5 years older than Emma, Andrews's daughter with Tony Walton.[citation needed]

Andrews continued working in television. In 1969 she shared the spotlight with singer Harry Belafonte for an NBC-TV special, *An Evening with Julie Andrews and Harry Belafonte*. In 1971 she appeared as a guest for the Grand Opening Special of Walt Disney World, and that same year she and Carol Burnett headlined a CBS special, *Julie and Carol At Lincoln Center*.

In 1972–73, Andrews starred in her own television variety series, *The Julie Andrews Hour*, on the ABC network. The show won seven Emmy Awards, but was cancelled after one season. Between 1973 and 1975, Andrews continued her association with ABC by headlining five variety specials for the network. She guest-starred on *The Muppet Show* in 1977 and appeared again with the Muppets on a CBS-TV special, *Julie Andrews: One Step Into Spring*, which aired in March, 1978.

In 1981 she appeared in Blake Edwards's *S.O.B.* (1981) in which she played Sally Miles, a character who agrees to "show my boobies" in a scene in the film-within-a-film.

In 1983 Andrews was chosen as the Hasty Pudding Woman of the Year by the Harvard University theatrical society. The roles of Victoria Grant and Count Victor Grezhinski in the film *Victor/Victoria* earned Andrews the 1983 Golden Globe Award for Best Actress – Motion Picture Musical or Comedy, as well as a nomination for the 1982 Academy Award for Best Actress, her third Oscar nomination.

In December 1987 Andrews starred in an ABC Christmas special, *Julie Andrews: The Sound Of Christmas*, which went on to win five Emmy Awards. Two years later she was reunited for the third time with Carol Burnett for a variety special which aired on ABC in December, 1989.

In 1991 Andrews made her television dramatic debut in the ABC made-for-TV movie, *Our Sons*, co-starring Ann-Margret.

In the summer of 1992 Andrews starred in her first television sitcom, *Julie*, which aired on ABC and co-starred James Farentino. In December 1992 she hosted the NBC holiday special, *Christmas In Washington*.

In 1993 she starred in a limited run at the Manhattan Theatre Club in the American premiere of Stephen Sondheim's revue, *Putting It Together*. Between 1994 and 1995 Andrews recorded two solo albums – the first saluted the music of Richard Rodgers and the second paid tribute to the words of Alan Jay Lerner. In 1995 she starred in the stage musical version of *Victor/Victoria*. It was her first appearance in a Broadway show in 35 years. Opening on Broadway on 25 October 1995 at the Marquis Theatre, it later went on the road on a world tour. When she was the only Tony Award nominee for the production, she declined the nomination saying that she could not accept because she felt the entire production was snubbed.

Miss Andrews was forced to quit the show towards the end of the Broadway run in 1997 when she developed vocal problems. She subsequently underwent surgery to remove non-cancerous nodules from her throat and was left unable to sing. In 1999 she filed a malpractice suit against the doctors at New York's Mount Sinai Hospital, including Dr. Scott Kessler and Dr. Jeffrey Libin, who had operated on her throat. Originally, the doctors assured the singing legend that she should regain her voice within six weeks, but Andrews's stepdaughter Jennifer Edwards said in 1999 "it's been two years, and it [her singing voice] still hasn't returned." The lawsuit was settled in September 2000.

Later that year Andrews was reunited with James Garner for the CBS made-for-TV movie, *One Special Night*, which aired in November 1999.

In the 2000 New Year's Millennium Honours List, Andrews was made a Dame Commander of the Order of the British Empire (DBE) for services to the performing arts. She also appears at #59 on the 2002 List of "100 Greatest Britons" sponsored by the BBC and chosen by the public.[citation needed]

In 2001 Andrews received Kennedy Center Honors. The same year she reunited with *Sound of Music* co-star Christopher Plummer in a live television performance of *On Golden Pond* (an adaptation of the 1979 play).

Career revival

In 2001 Andrews appeared in *The Princess Diaries*, her first Disney film since 1964's *Mary Poppins*. She starred as Queen Clarisse Marie Renaldi and reprised the role in a sequel, *The Princess Diaries 2: Royal Engagement* (2004). In *The Princess Diaries 2*, Andrews sang on film for the first time since having throat surgery. The song, "Your Crowning Glory", was set in a limited range of an octave to accommodate her recovering voice. The film's music supervisor, Dawn Soler, recalled that Andrews, "nailed the song on the first take. I looked around and I saw grips with tears in their eyes."

Andrews continued her association with Disney when she appeared as the nanny in two 2003 made-for-television movies based on the Eloise books, a series of children's books by Kay Thompson about a child who lives in the Plaza Hotel in New York City. *Eloise at the Plaza* premiered in April 2003, and *Eloise at Christmastime* was broadcast in November 2003. The same year she made her debut as a theatre director, directing a revival of *The Boy Friend*, the musical in which she made her 1954 Broadway debut, at the Bay Street Theatre in Sag Harbor, New York. Her production, which featured costume and scenic design by her former husband Tony Walton, was remounted at the Goodspeed Opera House in 2005 and went on a national tour in 2006.

From 2005 to 2006 Andrews served as the Official Ambassador for Disneyland's 18-month-long, 50th anniversary celebration, the "Happiest Homecoming on Earth", travelling to promote the celebration, and recording narration and appearing at several events at the park.

In 2004 Andrews performed the voice of Queen Lillian in the animated blockbuster *Shrek 2* (2004), reprising the role for its sequels, *Shrek the Third* (2007) and *Shrek Forever After* (2010). Later, in 2007, she narrated *Enchanted*, a live-action Disney musical comedy that both poked fun and paid homage to classic Disney films such as *Mary Poppins*.

In January 2007 Andrews was honoured with the Lifetime Achievement Award at the Screen Actors Guild's awards and stated that her goals included continuing to direct for the stage and possibly to produce her own Broadway musical. She published *Home: A Memoir of My Early Years*, which she characterised as "part one" of her autobiography, on 1 April 2008. *Home* chronicles her early years in UK's music hall circuit and ends in 1962 with her winning the role of Mary Poppins. For a Walt Disney video release she again portrayed Mary Poppins and narrated the story of *The Cat That Looked at a King* in 2004.

In July through early August 2008, Andrews hosted *Julie Andrews' The Gift of Music*, a short tour of the United States where she sang various Rodgers and Hammerstein songs and symphonised her recently published book, *Simeon's Gift*. These were her first public singing performances in a dozen years, due to her failed vocal cord surgery.

On May 8, 2009, Andrews received the honorary George and Ira Gershwin Award for Lifetime Achievement in Music at the annual UCLA Spring Sing competition in Pauley Pavilion. Receiving the award she remarked, "Go Bruins. Beat SC ... strike up the band to celebrate every one of those victories."

2010

On November 25, 2009, it was announced that "Andrews will be singing in a concert at The O2 Arena (London) on May 8, 2010. Accompanied by the Royal Philharmonic Orchestra and an ensemble of five performers, she will sing favourites from her stage and film career". However she appeared on British television on December 15, 2009, and said that rumours that she would be singing were not true. Instead, she said she will be doing a form of "speak singing".[citation needed]

In January 2010, for the second consecutive time, Andrews was the official USA presenter of the New Year's Day Vienna concert. Andrews also had a supporting role in the film *Tooth Fairy*, which opened to unfavourable reviews although the box office receipts were successful. On her promotion tour for the film she also spoke of *Operation USA* and the aid campaign to the Haiti disaster.

On May 8, 2010, Andrews made her London comeback after a 21-year absence (her last performance there was a Christmas concert at the Royal Festival Hall in 1989). The evening, though well received by the 20,000 fans present, who gave her standing ovation after standing ovation, did not convince the critics.

On May 18, 2010, Andrews' 23rd book (this one also written with her daughter Emma) was published. In June 2010 the book, entitled *The Very Fairy Princess*, reached number 1 on the New York Times Best Seller List for Children's Books.

On May 21, 2010, her film *Shrek Forever After* was released; in it Andrews reprises her role as the Queen.

On July 9, 2010, *Despicable Me*–an animated movie in which Andrews lent her voice to Marlena, the evil mother of the main character (Gru, voiced by Steve Carell)–opened to rave reviews and strong box office.

On August 29, 2010, the British press reports the news that a planned tribute for Andrews' 75th birthday, on a BBC television special, might not go ahead for a series of reasons that, at the moment, remain unclear.

Acting career

Film

Year	Title	Role	Notes
1949	*La Rosa di Bagdad*	Princess Zeila	dubbed voice for the 1967 English-language version
1964	*Mary Poppins*	Mary Poppins	Academy Award for Best Actress Golden Globe Award for Best Actress - Motion Picture Musical or Comedy
1964	*The Americanization of Emily*	Emily Barham	
1965	*Salzburg Sight and Sound*	Herself	short subject
1965	*The Sound of Music*	Maria von Trapp	Golden Globe Award for Best Actress - Motion Picture Musical or Comedy Nominated—Academy Award for Best Actress
1966	*Torn Curtain*	Dr. Sarah Louise Sherman	
1966	*Hawaii*	Jerusha Bromley	
1967	*Think Twentieth*	Herself	short subject
1967	*Thoroughly Modern Millie*	Millie Dillmount	Nominated - Golden Globe Award for Best Actress – Motion Picture Musical or Comedy
1968	*Star!*	Gertrude Lawrence	Nominated - Golden Globe Award for Best Actress – Motion Picture Musical or Comedy
1970	*Darling Lili*	Lili Smith (Schmidt)	Nominated - Golden Globe Award for Best Actress – Motion Picture Musical or Comedy
1971	*The Moviemakers*	Herself (uncredited)	short subject
1972	*Julie*	Herself	documentary
1974	*The Tamarind Seed*	Judith Farrow	
1979	*10*	Samantha Taylor	Nominated - Golden Globe Award for Best Actress - Motion Picture Musical or Comedy
1980	*Little Miss Marker*	Amanda	
1981	*S.O.B.*	Sally Miles	
1982	*Victor/Victoria*	Victor/Victoria	Golden Globe Award for Best Actress - Motion Picture Musical or Comedy Nominated—Academy Award for Best Actress
1982	*Trail of the Pink Panther*	Charwoman	uncredited
1983	*The Man Who Loved Women*	Marianna	

Year	Title	Role	Notes
1986	*That's Life!*	Gillian Fairchild	Nominated - Golden Globe Award for Best Actress - Motion Picture Musical or Comedy
1986	*Duet for One*	Stephanie Anderson	
1991	*A Fine Romance*	Mrs. Pamela Piquet	*Cin cin* – USA title
2000	*Relative Values*	Felicity Marshwood	
2001	*The Princess Diaries*	Queen Clarisse Renaldi	
2002	*Unconditional Love*	Herself	performer: *Getting to Know You*
2003	*Eloise at the Plaza*	Nanny	
2003	*Eloise at Christmastime*	Nanny	
2004	*Shrek 2*	Queen Lillian	voice
2004	*The Princess Diaries 2: Royal Engagement*	Queen Clarisse Renaldi	
2007	*Shrek the Third*	Queen Lillian	voice
2007	*Enchanted*	Narrator	voice
2010	*The Tooth Fairy*	Lily	
2010	*Shrek Forever After*	Queen Lillian	voice
2010	*Despicable Me*	Gru's Mom (Marlena)	voice
2011	*Enchanted 2*	Narrator	voice

Television

Year	Title	Role	Notes
1956	*Ford Star Jubilee*	Lise	*High Tor*
1957	*Rodgers and Hammerstein's Cinderella*	Cinderella	Original live broadcast, March 31
1959	*Hans Christian Andersen's The Gentle Flame*	Trissa	BBC broadcast December 25
1962	*Julie and Carol at Carnegie Hall*	Herself	
1965	*The Julie Andrews Show*	Host	
1969	*A World in Music*	Herself	"An Evening with Julie Andrews and Harry Belafonte"
1971	*Julie and Carol at Lincoln Center*	Herself	
1972–1973	*The Julie Andrews Hour*	Host	
1973	*Julie on Sesame Street*	Herself	

1974	Julie and Dick at Covent Garden	Herself	
1974	Julie and Jackie: How Sweet It Is	Herself	
1975	Julie: My Favorite Things	Herself	
1978	Julie Andrews: One Step Into Spring	Herself – host	
1987	Julie Andrews: The Sound of Christmas	Herself	
1989	Julie & Carol: Together Again	Herself	
1990	Julie Andrews in Concert	Herself	
1991	Our Sons	Audrey Grant	aka *Too Little, Too Late*
1992	Julie	Julie Carlisle	Series cancelled after 3 months
1993	Sound of Orchestra		
1999	One Special Night	Catherine	
2001	On Golden Pond	Ethel Thayer	
2001	Thomas and Friends	Old Slow Coach	voice
2003	Eloise at the Plaza	Nanny	
2003	Eloise at Christmastime	Nanny	
2009	Great Performances: "From Vienna: The New Year's Celebration 2009"	Herself	Narrator / Host, succeeding *Walter Cronkite*
2010	Todos contra Juan	Herself	Argentinian TV sitcom

Stage

Year	Title	Role	Notes
1954	The Boy Friend	Polly Brown	
1956	My Fair Lady	Eliza Doolittle	Nominated—Tony Award for Best Actress in a Musical
1961	Camelot	Queen Guinevere	Nominated—Tony Award for Best Actress in a Musical
1993	Putting It Together	Amy	
1995	Victor/Victoria	Victor/Victoria	Nominated—Tony Award for Best Actress in a Musical (nomination declined)

Honors

Honors

Year	Award	Category	Result	For
1955	Theatre World Award	Outstanding Broadway Debut	Won	*The Boy Friend*
1957	Tony Award	Best Actress in a Musical	Nominated	*My Fair Lady*
1957	Emmy Award	Best Actress in a Single Performance – Lead or Support	Nominated	*Rodgers and Hammerstein's Cinderella* (CBS)
1961	Tony Award	Best Actress in a Musical	Nominated	*Camelot*
1964	Academy Award	Best Actress	Won	*Mary Poppins*
1964	Golden Globe	Best Actress – Musical or Comedy	Won	*Mary Poppins*
1964	BAFTA	Most Promising Newcomer	Won	*Mary Poppins*
1964	Laurel Awards	Musical Performance, Female	Won	*Mary Poppins*
1964	Grammy Awards	Best Recording For Children	Won	*Mary Poppins (Album)*
1964–1965	Emmy Award	Individual Achievements in Entertainment (Actors and Performers)	Nominated	*The Andy Williams Show*
1965	Academy Award	Best Actress	Nominated	*The Sound of Music*
1965	Golden Globe	Best Actress – Musical or Comedy	Won	*The Sound of Music*
1965	BAFTA	Best British Actress	Nominated	*The Sound of Music*
1965	Laurel Awards	Musical Performance, Female	Won	*The Sound of Music*
1966	BAFTA	Best British Actress	Nominated	*The Americanization of Emily*
1967	Golden Globe	Best Actress – Musical or Comedy	Nominated	*Thoroughly Modern Millie*
1967	Golden Globe	Henrietta Award – World Film Favorite – Female	Won	
1967	Laurel Awards	Female Comedy Performance	Won	*Thoroughly Modern Millie*
1967	Laurel Awards	Female Star	Won	
1968	Golden Globe	Best Actress – Musical or Comedy	Nominated	*Star!*
1968	Golden Globe	Henrietta Award – World Film Favorite – Female	Won	
1970	Golden Globe	Best Actress – Musical or comedy	Nominated	*Darling Lili*

1972	Emmy Award	Outstanding Single Program – Variety or Musical – Variety and Popular Music	Nominated	*Julie and Carol at Lincoln Center*
1973	Golden Globes	Best Motion Picture Actress – Musical/Comedy	Nominated	*The Julie Andrews Hour*
1973	Emmy Awards	Outstanding Variety Musical Series	Won	*The Julie Andrews Hour*
1979	Golden Globe	Best actress – Musical or Comedy	Nominated	*10*
1980–1981	Emmy Award	Individual Achievement in Children's Programming (Performers)	Nominated	*Julie Andrews' Invitation to the Dance with Rudolph Nureyev (The CBS Festival of Lively Arts For Young People)*
1982	Academy Award	Best Actress	Nominated	*Victor/Victoria*
1982	Golden Globe	Best Actress – Musical or Comedy	Won	*Victor/Victoria*
1983	Hasty Pudding Theatricals	Woman of the Year	Won	
1983	People's Choice Award	Film Acting	Won	
1986	Golden Globe	Best Actress – Musical or Comedy	Nominated	*That's Life!*
1986	Golden Globe	Best Actress – Drama	Nominated	*Duet for One*
1995	Emmy Awards	Outstanding Individual Performance in a Variety or Music Program	Nominated	*The Sound of Julie Andrews*
1996	Tony Award	Best Actress in a Musical	Nominated	*Victor/Victoria*
1996	Grammy Award	Best Traditional Pop Vocal Performance	Nominated	"Broadway: The Music Of Richard Rodgers"
2001	Kennedy Center Honors	Kennedy Center Honoree	Won	
2001	Society of Singers	Society of Singers Life Achievement	Won	*Lifetime Achievement*
2001	Donostia Award	San Sebastian International Film Festival	Won	*Lifetime Achievement*
2004	Emmy Awards	Supporting Actress, Miniseries or a Movie	Nominated	*Eloise at Christmastime*
2005	Emmy Awards	Outstanding Nonfiction Series	Won	*Broadway: The American Musical*
2006	Screen Actors Guild	Life Achievement Award	Won	*Lifetime Achievement*
2009	UCLA George and Ira Gershwin Award	Lifetime Musical Achievement	Won	*Lifetime Musical Achievement*

Bibliography

Andrews has published books under her name as well as the pen names Julie Andrews Edwards and Julie Edwards.

- Andrews, Julie. *Home: A Memoir of My Early Years* (2008) Hyperion ISBN 0786865652
- Edwards, Julie Andrews (Author) and Johanna Westerman (Illustrator). *Mandy* [1]. HarperTrophy 1989. ISBN 0064402967.
- Edwards, Julie. *The Last of the Really Great Whangdoodles* [2]. New York: Harper and Row. 1974. ISBN 000184461X.
- Edwards, Julie Andrews. *Little Bo: The Story of Bonnie Boadicea* [3]. Hyperion, 1999. ISBN 0-7868-0514-5. (several others in this series.)
- Edwards, Julie Andrews and Emma Walton Hamilton. *Dumpy the Dumptruck* [4]. Hyperion, 2000. ISBN 0-7868-0609-5. (several others in the Dumpy series.)
- Edwards, Julie Andrews and Emma Walton Hamilton, (Authors). Gennady Spirin (Illustrator). *Simeon's Gift* [5]. 2003. ISBN 0-06-008914-8.
- Edwards, Julie Andrews and Emma Walton Hamilton. *Dragon: Hound of Honor* [6]. HarperTrophy, 2005. ISBN 0-06-057121-7.
- Edwards, Julie Andrews and Emma Walton Hamilton (Authors) and Tony Walton (Illustrator). *The Great American Mousical* [7]. HarperTrophy, 2006. ISBN 0-06-057918-8.
- Edwards, Julie Andrews and Emma Walton Hamilton. *Thanks to You: Wisdom from Mother and Child* [8]. Julie Andrews Collection, 2007. ISBN 0061240028.

External links

- Julie Andrews [9] at the Internet Movie Database
- Julie Andrews [10] at the TCM Movie Database
- Julie Andrews [11] at the Internet Broadway Database
- Julie Andrews [12] at the Internet Off-Broadway Database
- Julie Andrews: Prim and Improper [13]
- The American Musical, Stars Over Broadway – Julie Andrews (PBS) [14]
- Julie Andrews [15] at the British Film Institute's Screenonline
- Works by or about Julie Andrews [16] in libraries (WorldCat catalog)

1. REDIRECT Template:Navboxes

Tony Curtis

	Tony Curtis
	Tony Curtis in 1955
Born	Bernard Schwartz June 3, 1925 Bronx, New York, United States
Died	September 29, 2010 (aged 85) Henderson, Nevada, United States
Occupation	Actor
Years active	1948–2010
Spouse	Janet Leigh (m. 1951–1962) (divorced) Christine Kaufmann (m. 1963–1967) (divorced) Leslie Allen (m. 1968–1982) (divorced) Andria Savio (m. 1983–1992) (divorced) Lisa Deutsch (m. 1993–1994) (divorced) Jill Vandenberg (m. 1998–2010) (his death)
Children	6, Kelly Curtis(1956), Jamie Lee Curtis (1958), Alexandra Curtis (1964), Allegra Curtis (1966), Nicolas (1972-1994) and Benjamin (1973)

Tony Curtis (June 3, 1925 – September 29, 2010) was an American film actor whose career spanned six decades, but had his greatest popularity during the 1950s and early 1960s. He acted in over 60 films in roles covering a wide range of genres, from light comedy to serious drama. In his later years, Curtis made numerous television appearances.

Although his early film roles were partly the result of his good looks, by the latter half of the 1950s he became a notable and strong screen presence. He began proving himself to be a "fine dramatic actor," having the range to act in numerous dramatic and comedy roles. In his earliest parts he acted in a string of "mediocre" films, including swashbucklers, westerns, light comedies, sports films, and a musical. However, by the time he starred in *Houdini* (1953) with his wife Janet Leigh, "his first clear success," notes critic David Thomson, his acting had progressed immensely.

He won his first serious recognition as a skilled dramatic actor in *Sweet Smell of Success* (1957) with co-star Burt Lancaster. The following year he was nominated for an Oscar for Best Actor in another drama, *The Defiant Ones* (1958). Curtis then gave what many believe was his best acting, in a completely different role, the comedy *Some Like it Hot* (1959). Thomson calls it an "outrageous film," and it was voted the number 1 funniest film in history from a survey done by the American Film Institute. It costarred Jack Lemmon and Marilyn Monroe, and was directed by Billy Wilder. That was followed by Blake Edwards' comedy *Operation Petticoat* (1959) with Cary Grant. They were both "frantic comedies," and displayed "his impeccable comic timing." He would collaborate with Edwards often on later films.

His most significant serious part came in 1968 when he starred in the true-life drama *The Boston Strangler*, which some consider his "last major film role." The part reinforced his reputation as a serious actor with his "chilling portrayal" of serial killer Albert de Salvo. He gained 30 pounds and had his face "rebuilt" with a false nose to look like the real de Salvo.

Curtis was the father of actresses Jamie Lee Curtis and Kelly Curtis who he fathered with his wife, actress Janet Leigh.

Early life

Curtis was born **Bernard Schwartz** in the Bronx, New York, the son of Emanuel Schwartz and Helen Klein. His parents were Hungarian Jewish immigrants from Mátészalka, Hungary. Hungarian was Curtis' only language until he was five or six, postponing his schooling. His father was a tailor and the family lived in the back of the shop — the parents in one corner and Curtis and his brothers Julius and Robert in another. His mother had once made an appearance as a participant on the television show *You Bet Your Life*, hosted by Groucho Marx. Curtis said, "When I was a child, Mom beat me up and was very aggressive and antagonistic." His mother was later diagnosed with schizophrenia, a mental illness which also affected his brother Robert and led to Robert's institutionalization.

When Curtis was eight, he and his younger brother Julius were placed in an orphanage for a month because their parents could not afford to feed them. Four years later, Julius was struck and killed by a truck. Curtis joined a neighborhood gang whose main crimes were playing hooky from school or minor pilfering at the local dime store. When he turned 11, a friendly neighbor saved him from what he feels would have led to a life of delinquency, by sending him to a Boy Scout camp, where he was able to settle down and work off his energy. He attended Seward Park High School and received his first bit part in a stage play at age 16.

He enlisted in the United States Navy after Pearl Harbor was bombed and war was declared. Having been inspired by Cary Grant's role in *Destination Tokyo* and Tyrone Power in *Crash Dive* (1943), he chose submarine duty and served aboard USS *Proteus*, a submarine tender. From his sub tender's signal bridge, he witnessed the Japanese surrender in Tokyo Bay from about a mile away. Following his discharge, Curtis attended City College of New York under the G.I. Bill and studied acting at the

Dramatic Workshop of The New School in New York with the influential German stage director Erwin Piscator, along with Elaine Stritch, Walter Matthau, and Rod Steiger. He was discovered by a talent agent and casting director Joyce Selznick. Curtis claims it was because he "was the handsomest of the boys."[citation needed] Arriving in Hollywood in 1948 at age 23, he was placed under contract at Universal Pictures and changed his name to Tony Curtis, taking his first name from the novel *Anthony Adverse* and his last name from "Kurtz", a surname from his mother's family. Although the studio taught him fencing and riding, Curtis admitted he was at first only interested in girls and money.[citation needed] Nonetheless, he was not hopeful of his chances in becoming a major actor, and feared having to return to the Bronx, a failure. He writes,

> I was a million-to-one shot, the *least* likely to succeed. I wasn't low man on the totem pole, I was *under* the totem pole, in a sewer, tied to a sack.

Career

Curtis's uncredited screen debut came in *Criss Cross* (1949) playing a rumba dancer. In his second film, *City Across the River* (also in 1949), he was credited as "Anthony Cross". Later, as "Tony Curtis", he cemented his reputation with breakthrough performances such as in the role of the scheming press agent Sidney Falco in *Sweet Smell of Success* (1957) with Burt Lancaster (who also starred in *Criss Cross*) and an Oscar-nominated performance as a bigoted escaped convict chained to Sidney Poitier in *The Defiant Ones*.

He did both screen comedy and drama, and became one of the most sought after stars in Hollywood. Curtis' comedies include *Some Like It Hot* (1959), *Sex and the Single Girl* (1964) and *The Great Race* (1965), and his dramas included playing the slave Antoninus in Stanley Kubrick's *Spartacus* (1960) co-starring Kirk Douglas and Sir Laurence Olivier, *The Outsider* (1961), the true story of WW II veteran Ira Hayes, and *The Boston Strangler* (1968), in which he played the self-confessed murderer of the film's title, Albert DeSalvo. The latter film was praised for Curtis' performance. He was also part of the all-star ensemble in Elia Kazan's 1976 drama *The Last Tycoon*.

Curtis appeared frequently on television; he co-starred with Roger Moore in the TV series *The Persuaders!*. Later, he co-starred in *McCoy* and *Vega$*. In the early 1960s, he was immortalized as "Stony Curtis," a voice-over guest star on *The Flintstones*.

Throughout his life, Curtis enjoyed painting, and since the early 1980s, painted as a second career. His work commands more than $25,000 a canvas now. In the last years of his life, he concentrated on painting rather than movies. A surrealist, Curtis claimed "Van Gogh, [Paul] Matisse, Picasso, Magritte" as influences. "I still make movies but I'm not that interested in them any more. But I paint all the time." In 2007, his painting *The Red Table* was on display in the Metropolitan Museum of Art in New York City. His paintings can also be seen at the Tony Vanderploeg Gallery in Carmel, California.

Curtis spoke of his disappointment at never being awarded an Oscar. But in March 2006, Curtis did receive the Sony Ericsson Empire Lifetime Achievement Award. He also has a star on the Hollywood Walk of Fame, and received the *Ordre des Arts et des Lettres* (Order of Arts and Letters) from France in 1995.

Personal life

Marriages and children

Curtis was married six times. His first wife was actress Janet Leigh, to whom he was married from 1951 to 1962, and with whom he fathered actresses Kelly and Jamie Lee Curtis. "For a while, we were Hollywood's golden couple," he said. "I was very dedicated and devoted to Janet, and on top of my trade, but in her eyes that goldenness started to wear off. I realized that whatever I was, I wasn't enough for Janet. That hurt me a lot and broke my heart."Wikipedia:Citing sources#When quoting someone

The studio they were both under contract with, Universal-International, generally stayed out of their stars' love lives. However, when they chose to get married, the studio executives spent 3 days trying to talk him out of it, telling him he would be "poisoning himself at the box office." They threatened "banishment" back to the Bronx and the end of his budding career. In response, Curtis and Leigh decided to defy the studio heads and instead eloped and were married by a local judge in Greenwich Connecticut. Comedian and close friend Jerry Lewis came as a witness.

It was Janet Leigh's third marriage. They divorced in 1962, and Curtis soon married Christine Kaufmann, the 17-year-old German co-star of his latest film, *Taras Bulba*. He stated that his marriage with Leigh had effectively ended "a year earlier". In 1963 Curtis married Kaufmann. They had two daughters, Alexandra (born July 19, 1964) and Allegra (born July 11, 1966). They divorced in 1968. Kaufmann resumed her career, which she had interrupted during her marriage.

Curtis was also married to:

- Leslie Allen (April 20, 1968 – 1982); divorced, two sons: Nicholas Curtis and Benjamin Curtis (born May 2,1973)
- Andria Savio (1983 – 1992); B movie actress (e.g. 1983's *Stryker*)
- Lisa Deutsch (February 28, 1993 – 1994); divorced
- Jill Vandenberg Curtis (November 6, 1998 – September 29, 2010; his death)

His last wife was 42 years his junior. They met in a restaurant in 1993 and married in 1998. "The age gap doesn't bother us. We laugh a lot. My body is functioning and everything is good. She's the sexiest woman I've ever known. We don't think about time. I don't use Viagra either. There are 50 ways to please your lover."Wikipedia:Citing sources#When quoting someone

His son Nicholas (December 31, 1970 — April 2, 1994, with Leslie Allen) died of a heroin overdose at the age of 23. Of this Curtis said, "As a father you don't recover from that. There isn't a moment at night that I don't remember him."Wikipedia:Citing sources#When quoting someone

According to the Pittsburgh-Post Gazette, Curtis, who had a problem with alcoholism and drug abuse, went though the treatment center of the Betty Ford Clinic in the mid 1980s, which did work for him.

Philanthropy

Beginning in 1990, Curtis and his daughter Jamie Lee Curtis took a renewed interest in their family's Hungarian-Jewish heritage, and helped finance the rebuilding of the "Great Synagogue" in Budapest, Hungary. The largest synagogue in Europe today, it was originally built in 1859 and suffered damage during World War II. In 1998, he also founded the Emanuel Foundation for Hungarian Culture, and served as honorary chairperson. The organization works for the restoration and preservation of synagogues and 1300 Jewish cemeteries in Hungary. He dedicated this to the 600,000 Jewish victims of the Holocaust in Hungary and lands occupied by the Hungarian Army. He also helped promote Hungary's national image in commercials.

Books and appearances

In 1994, a mural featuring his likeness, painted by the artist George Sportelli, was unveiled on the Sunset Boulevard overpass of the Hollywood Freeway Highway 101 in California.

In 2004, he was inducted into the University of Nevada, Las Vegas Hall of Fame. A street is named after him in the Sun City Anthem development in Henderson, Nevada.[*citation needed*]

In 2008, he was featured in the documentary *The Jill & Tony Curtis Story* about his efforts with his wife to rescue horses from slaughterhouses.

Curtis, during a signing of his 2008 memoir, *American Prince*

In October 2008, Curtis's autobiography *American Prince: A Memoir*, was published. In it, he describes his encounters with other Hollywood legends of the time including Frank Sinatra and James Dean, as well as his hard-knock childhood and path to success. It was followed by the publication of his next book, *The Making of Some Like it Hot: My Memories of Marilyn Monroe and the Classic American Movie* (2009). Curtis shared his memories of the making of the movie, in particular about Marilyn Monroe, whose antics and attitude on the set made everyone miserable.

On May 22, 2009, Curtis apologized to the BBC radio audience after he used three profanities in a six-minute interview with BBC presenter William Crawley. The presenter also apologized to the audience for Curtis's "Hollywood realism". Curtis explained that he thought the interview was being taped, when it was in fact live.

Illnesses and death

In 1984 Curtis was rushed to hospital suffering from advanced cirrhosis as a result of his alcoholism and cocaine addiction. He then entered the Betty Ford Clinic and vowed to overcome his "various illnesses". He underwent heart bypass surgery in 1994.

Curtis nearly died when he contracted pneumonia in December 2006 and was in a coma for several days. As a result he used a wheelchair and could only walk short distances.

On July 8, 2010, Curtis, who suffered from chronic obstructive pulmonary disease (COPD), was hospitalized in Las Vegas after suffering an asthma attack during a book signing engagement in Henderson, Nevada at Costco.

Curtis died at his Henderson, Nevada home on September 29, 2010, of cardiac arrest. In a release to the Associated Press, his daughter, actress Jamie Lee Curtis, stated:

> "My father leaves behind a legacy of great performances in movies and in his paintings and assemblages. He leaves behind children and their families who loved him and respected him and a wife and in-laws who were devoted to him. He also leaves behind fans all over the world. He will be greatly missed."

He was interred at Palm Memorial Park Cemetery in Green Valley, Nevada on October 4, 2010. His memorial service was attended by his daughter, Jamie Lee Curtis, Arnold Schwarzenegger, Ron Jeremy, and Vera Goulet. Investor Kirk Kerkorian, actor Kirk Douglas and singer Phyllis McGuire were among the honorary pallbearers.

Filmography

- *Criss Cross* (1949)
- *City Across the River* (1949)
- *The Lady Gambles* (1949)
- *Take One False Step* (1949) (scenes deleted)
- *Johnny Stool Pigeon* (1949)
- *How to Smuggle a Hernia Across the Border* (1949) (short subject)
- *Woman in Hiding* (1950)
- *Francis* (1950)
- *I Was a Shoplifter* (1950)
- *Sierra* (1950)
- *Winchester '73* (1950) (Credited as Anthony Curtis)
- *On My Way to the Crusades, I Met a Girl Who...* (1968)
- *Rosemary's Baby* (1968) (voice)
- *The Boston Strangler* (1968)
- *Monte Carlo or Bust* (1969)
- *You Can't Win 'Em All* (1970)
- *Suppose They Gave a War and Nobody Came?* (1970)
- *The Persuaders!* (1971–1972)
- *Mission: Monte Carlo* (1974)
- *Lepke* (1975)
- *The Count of Monte Cristo* (1975)
- *London Conspiracy* (1976)

- *Kansas Raiders* (1950)
- *The Prince Who Was a Thief* (1951)
- *Meet Danny Wilson* (1952) (cameo)
- *Flesh and Fury* (1952)
- *No Room for the Groom* (1952)
- *Son of Ali Baba* (1952)
- *Houdini* (1953)
- *The All-American* (1953)
- *Forbidden* (1953)
- *Beachhead* (1954)
- *Johnny Dark* (1954)
- *The Black Shield of Falworth* (1954)
- *Six Bridges to Cross* (1955)
- *So This Is Paris* (1955)
- *The Purple Mask* (1955)
- *The Rawhide Years* (1955)
- *The Square Jungle* (1955)
- *Trapeze* (1956)
- *Mister Cory* (1957)
- *Sweet Smell of Success* (1957)
- *The Midnight Story* (1957)
- *The Vikings* (1958)
- *Kings Go Forth* (1958)
- *The Defiant Ones* (1958)
- *The Perfect Furlough* (1958)
- *Some Like It Hot* (1959)
- *Operation Petticoat* (1959)
- *Who Was That Lady?* (1960)
- *The Rat Race* (1960)
- *Spartacus* (1960)
- *Pepe* (1960) (cameo)
- *The Great Impostor* (1961)
- *The Outsider* (1961), as Ira Hayes
- *Taras Bulba* (1962)
- *40 Pounds of Trouble* (1962)
- *The List of Adrian Messenger* (1963) (cameo)
- *Captain Newman, M.D.* (1963)
- *Paris, When It Sizzles* (1964) (cameo)
- *Wild and Wonderful* (1964)
- *The Last Tycoon* (1976)
- *Casanova & Co.* (1977)
- *Sextette* (1978)
- *The Manitou* (1978)
- *The Bad News Bears Go to Japan* (1978)
- *The Users* (1978)
- *Electric Light Orchestra Out of the Blue: Live at Wembley* (1978)
- *Double Take* (1979)
- *Title Shot* (1979)
- *Little Miss Marker* (1980)
- *It Rained All Night the Day I Left* (1980)
- *The Mirror Crack'd* (1980)
- *Moviola: The Scarlett O'Hara War* (1980)
- *Othello, the Black Commando* (1982)
- *Where Is Parsifal?* (1983)
- *BrainWaves* (1983)
- *The Fantasy Film Worlds of George Pal* (1985) (documentary)
- *Club Life* (1985)
- *Insignificance* (1985)
- *The Last of Philip Banter* (1986)
- *Balboa* (1986)
- *The Passenger - Welcome to Germany* (1988)
- *Lobster Man From Mars* (1989)
- *Midnight* (1989)
- *Tarzan in Manhattan* (1989)
- *Walter & Carlo In America* (1989)
- *Prime Target* (1991)
- *Center of the Web* (1992)
- *Hugh Hefner: Once Upon a Time* (1992) (documentary)
- *Naked in New York* (1993)
- *The Mummy Lives* (1993)
- *A Century of Cinema* (1994) (documentary)
- *The Immortals* (1995)
- *The Celluloid Closet* (1995) (documentary)
- *Roseanne* - TV Series (1996) (role as Hal, ballroom dance studio instructor)
- *Hardball* (1997)
- *Brittle Glory* (1997)
- *Elvis Meets Nixon* (1997)
- *Alien X Factor* (1997)

- *Goodbye Charlie* (1964)
- *Sex and the Single Girl* (1964)
- *The Great Race* (1965)
- *Boeing Boeing* (1965)
- *The Flintstones* (1965) (voice)
- *Chamber of Horrors* (1966) (cameo)
- *Not with My Wife, You Don't!* (1966)
- *Arrivederci, Baby!* (1966)
- *Don't Make Waves* (1967)
- *Stargames* (1998)
- *Louis & Frank* (1998)
- *Play It to the Bone* (1999) (cameo)
- *Reflections of Evil* (2002) (narrator)
- *Where's Marty?* (2006)
- *The Blacksmith and the Carpenter* (2007) (voice)
- *David & Fatima* (2008)
- *The Jill & Tony Curtis Story* (2008) (documentary feature)

Further reading

- Curtis, Tony; Barry Paris (1993). *Tony Curtis: The Autobiography*. New York: William Morrow & Company. ISBN 978-0-688-09759-2.
- Ayres, Ian (2006). *Van Gogh's Ear: The Celebrity Edition (includes Tony Curtis's prose/poetry/artwork)*. Paris: French Connection. ISBN 978-2-914-85307-1.
- Curtis, Tony; Peter Golenbock (2008). *Tony Curtis: American Prince: My Autobiography*. New York: Harmony Books. ISBN 978-0-307-40849-5.
- Curtis, Tony (2009). *Some Like it Hot: My Memories of Marilyn Monroe and the Making of the Classic Movie*. New York: John Wiley & Sons. p. 240. ISBN 978-0470537213.

External links

- CBS news: Tony Curtis 1925-2010 [1] video: 1.5 minutes
- Tony Curtis [2] at the Internet Movie Database
- Tony Curtis [3] at the TCM Movie Database
- Tony Curtis [4] at Find a Grave
- Biography [5] and naval service [6] from the California Center for Military History website
- Tony Curtis' Famous Friends [7] - slideshow by *Life magazine*
- 2009 interview [8] with Dodd Vickers for the Magic Newswire [9]
- 2007 interview [10] by Nick Thomas in Nevada Magazine
- Tony Curtis and Nehemiah Persoff talk [11] about Some Like it Hot
- John Patterson, *Some like it very hot (Interview),* The Guardian, 18 April 2008 [12]
- Alison Jackson, *Some tormented Hollywood souls still like their gossip hot, Profile: Tony Curtis,* Sunday Times, 20 April 2008 [13]
- Documentary film, *The Jill & Tony Curtis Story* [14]
- Photographs and literature [15]
- Tony Curtis: Life and Times [16] - slideshow by *Life magazine*
- The Telegraph Obituary [17]

TV Appearances

Mister Ed

	*Mister Ed*
	*Mister Ed* title, from a colorized print
Genre	Sitcom
Created by	Walter R. Brooks
Directed by	Jus Addiss Rodney Amateau Arthur Lubin John Rich Ira Stewart Alan Young
Starring	Alan Young Connie Hines
Voices of	Allan "Rocky" Lane
Theme music composer	Ray Evans Jay Livingston
Opening theme	"Mr. Ed" by Jay Livingston
Composer(s)	Jack Cookerly Dave Kahn
Country of origin	United States
Language(s)	English
No. of seasons	6
No. of episodes	143
	**Production**
Executive producer(s)	Al Simon
Producer(s)	Arthur Lubin
Cinematography	Archie R. Dalzell Maury Gertsman
Running time	30 mins.

Production company(s)	The Mister Ed Company
Distributor	Filmways Television
Broadcast	
Original channel	Syndication (1961) CBS (1961–1966)
Original run	January 5, 1961 – February 6, 1966
Chronology	
Related shows	*Mister Ed* (2004)

Mister Ed is an American television situation comedy produced by Filmways that first aired in syndication from January 5 to July 2, 1961 and then on CBS from October 1, 1961 to February 6, 1966. *Mister Ed* was the first series ever to debut as a midseason replacement.

The stars of the show are Mister Ed, an intelligent palomino horse who could talk ("played" by gelding Bamboo Harvester and voiced by Allan Lane), and his owner, an eccentric and enormously klutzy architect named Wilbur Post (portrayed by Alan Young). Much of the program's humor stemmed from the fact Mister Ed would speak only to Wilbur, as well as Ed's notoriety as a troublemaker. According to the show's producer, Arthur Lubin, Young was chosen as the lead character because he "just seemed like the sort of guy a horse would talk to." Lubin, a friend of Mae West, scored a coup by persuading the screen icon to guest star in one episode.

In the United States, reruns aired on Nick at Nite from March 3, 1986 to February 1, 1993. Sister station TV Land also reran the show from 1996 to 1998 and again from 2003 to 2006. The series is currently broadcast every morning on This TV, along with sister series *The Patty Duke Show*.

Beginnings

The show was derived from short stories by Walter R. Brooks, including *Ed Takes the Pledge*. Brooks is otherwise known for the *Freddy the Pig* series of children's novels, which likewise feature talking animals who interact with humans.

The concept of the show was similar to *Francis the Talking Mule*, with the equine normally talking only to one person (Wilbur), and thus both helping and frustrating its owner.

Mister Ed

The first horse that played Mister Ed for the pilot episode was a chestnut gelding. However, the permanent equine star of the show was Bamboo Harvester (1949–1970), a crossbred gelding of American Saddlebred, Arabian and grade ancestry.

Mister Ed the horse was voiced by ex-B-movie cowboy star Allan "Rocky" Lane (speaking) and Sheldon Allman (singing, except his line in the theme song, which was sung by its composer, Jay Livingston).

Ed was voice-trained for the show by Les Hilton. Lane remained anonymous as the voice of Mister Ed, and the show's producers referred to him only as "an actor who prefers to remain nameless," though once the show became a hit, Lane campaigned the producers for credit, which he never received. The credits listed Mister Ed as playing "Himself"; however, his family tree name was Bamboo Harvester. Ed's stablemate, a quarter horse named *Pumpkin*, who was later to appear in the television series *Green Acres*, was also Ed's stunt double in the show.

Death

By 1968, Bamboo Harvester was suffering from a variety of health problems. In 1970 he was euthanized with no publicity, and buried at Snodgrass Farm in Oklahoma. However, a different version was given by Alan Young. Young wrote that he'd frequently visit his former "co-star" in retirement. He states that Mr. Ed died from an inadvertent tranquilizer administered while he was "in retirement" in a stable in Burbank, California where he lived with his trainer Lester Hilton. Young says Hilton was out of town visiting relatives and a temporary care giver might have seen Ed rolling on the ground, struggling to get up. Young said Ed was a heavy horse and he wasn't always strong enough to get back on his feet without struggling. The theory is the care giver thought the horse was in distress and administered a tranquilizer and for unknown reason, the horse died within hours. The remains were cremated and scattered by Hilton in the Los Angeles area at a spot known only to him.

A different horse that died in Oklahoma in February 1979 was widely thought to be Bamboo Harvester, but this horse was in fact a horse that posed for the still pictures of "Mr. Ed" used by the production company for the show's press kits. After Bamboo Harvester's death in 1970, this horse was unofficially known as Mister Ed, which led to him being reported as such (including sardonic comments on *Saturday Night Live's* Weekend Update) following his own death.

Young said when the Oklahoma horse death story came out in 1979, he knew it wasn't the real Mr. Ed, but didn't have the heart to "shatter their illusions" that the horse being memorialized wasn't the real Mr. Ed. He believes it was a horse used for early publicity photos. There are conflicting stories involving of the death of Bamboo Harvester, the horse that played Mr. Ed.

Other characters

The other main characters in the show were Wilbur's tolerant young wife, Carol (Connie Hines); and their friendly neighbors the Addisons, Roger (Larry Keating) and Kay (Edna Skinner) until 1963 (upon Larry Keating's death that year) and then the Kirkwoods, Gordon (Leon Ames) and Winnie (Florence MacMichael). In 1963, the child actor Darby Hinton, cast thereafter as Israel Boone on NBC's *Daniel Boone*, guest starred as Rocky in the episode "Getting Ed's Goat". Jack Albertson appeared occasionally from 1961 to 1963 as Kay Addison's older brother Paul Fenton.

For the final season, the show focused strictly on the home life of the Posts, which was made more interesting when Carol's grumpy and uptight father, Mr. Higgins (Barry Kelly), who appeared occasionally throughout the entire series, apparently moved in with Wilbur and Carol during the final episodes. Mr. Higgins loathed Wilbur since Wilbur's quirky eccentricity always clashed with his own emotionless and uptight personality, and he never stopped trying to persuade Carol to leave Wilbur, whom he referred to as a "kook" because of his clumsyness.

Although Connie Hines retired from acting a few years after the show's cancellation in 1966, she and Alan Young made public appearances together.

Theme song

The theme song was written by the songwriting team of Jay Livingston and Ray Evans and sung, for the show, by Livingston, who was not the first choice. Only the music was used to open the first six episodes, but when a professional singer could not be found, Livingston agreed to sing the lyrics, because the producers were so pleased with his vocals, and he was never replaced.

Sponsorship

The series was sponsored from 1961 to 1963 by Studebaker Corporation, a now-defunct American car manufacturer. Studebakers were featured prominently in the show during this period. The Posts are shown owning a 1962 Lark convertible, and the company used publicity shots featuring the Posts and Mister Ed with their product (various cast members also appeared in "integrated commercials" for Lark at the end of the program). The Addisons are shown owning a 1963 Avanti. Ford Motor Company provided the vehicles starting at the beginning of 1965. It is also interesting to note that, in the first episode ever aired, the Posts were driving a 1961 Studebaker Lark.

Remake

In 2004, a remake was planned for the Fox network, with Sherman Hemsley as the voice of Mister Ed, David Alan Basche as Wilbur, Sherilyn Fenn as Carol, and Sara Paxton. The pilot was filmed, but was not picked up by Fox. The show's writer and producer, Drake Sather, committed suicide shortly before the pilot's completion.

Making Ed "talk"

It is often said the crew was able to get Mister Ed to move his mouth by applying peanut butter to his gums in order for him to try to remove it by moving his lips. However, Alan Young said in 2004 that he had started the story himself. In another interview, Young said, "Al Simon and Arthur Lubin, the producers, suggested we keep the method a secret because they thought kids would be disappointed if they found out the technical details of how it was done, so I made up the peanut butter story, and everyone bought it. It was initially done by putting a piece of nylon thread in his mouth. But Ed actually learned to move his lips on cue when the trainer touched his hoof. In fact, he soon learned to do it when I stopped talking during a scene! Ed was very smart."

Others argued that examination of Mister Ed footage shows Ed's handler pulling strings to make him talk, and that this method was at work at least some of the time. Young later said during an interview for the Archive of American Television that a nylon string was tied to the halter and the loose end inserted under his lip to make Ed talk, saying that he had used the peanut butter fable for years in radio interviews instead of telling the truth. The loose thread can be seen tied to the halter, and it is clearly not taut as it would be if it were being pulled. Young also states in the AAT interview that after the first season, Ed didn't need the nylon – Alan and trainer Les were out riding one day and Les started laughing, telling Alan to look at Ed, who was moving his lips every time they stopped talking, as if attempting to join in the conversation. This difference is visible when comparing first season episodes to later ones, as it is clear that early on he's working the irritating string out, sometimes working his tongue in the attempt too, and later on he tends to only move his upper lip, and appears to watch Alan Young closely, waiting for him to finish his lines before twitching his lip.

Young added in the Archive interview that Ed saw the trainer as the disciplinarian, or father figure, and when scolded for missing a cue, would go to Alan for comfort, like a mother figure, which Les said was a good thing.

Cast

Main cast:
Allan Lane (voice only) ... Mister Ed
Alan Young ... Wilbur Post
Connie Hines ... Carol Post

Supporting Cast:
Larry Keating ... Roger Addison (1961–1963); Seasons 1–3
Edna Skinner ... Kay Addison (1961–1963); Seasons 1–4
Leon Ames ... Gordon Kirkwood (1963–1965); Seasons 4–5
Florence MacMichael ... Winnie Kirkwood (1963–1965); Seasons 4–5
Jack Albertson ... Paul Fenton (occasionally 1961–1963); Seasons 2–4
Barry Kelly ... Carol's Father, Mr. Higgins (occasionally 1962–1966)

Housing development

In 2007 it was reported that a builder intended to create a community near Tahlequah, Oklahoma built around the supposed final resting place (although that fact is disputable) of Mister Ed. It is intended to be themed to the style of the show and its period.

Appearances in other media

- *Histeria!* featured a recurring character in the form of a talking horse who spoke very much like Mister Ed. One episode, "20th Century Presidents", also a theme song parodying that of *Mister Ed*.
- The Beastie Boys use a sample of Mister Ed's voice in their song Time To Get Ill from the album Licensed to Ill.
- The song "Mr. Klaw" by They Might Be Giants features lyrics based on those of the show's theme.
- "Now That I Am Dead" by French Frith Kaiser Thompson features a "Mister Ed" impersonation on the line "I am Mister Dead."
- British sketch comedy show *Harry Enfield's Television Programme* featured a Grotesque character called Mister Dead, a talking human corpse who travels around with his living friend and often helps him get out of troublesome situations, such as in one sketch where he avoids a speeding ticket by pretending to rush Mister Dead to the mortuary.
- In the episode of the same name of Mr. Show, David finds a "talking junkie named Mister Junkie", in a sketch that parodies Mister Ed, including a parody of the theme song.
- A Tribute Music CD called *Mister Ed Unplugged* was released, featuring new recordings of the "Theme From Mister Ed" and longer versions of "The Pretty Little Filly" and "Empty Feedbag Blues", which were both written by the late Sheldon Allman, who was also the original singing voice of Mister Ed.
- Dell Comics published Mister Ed in Four Color # 1295
- In the show Dinosaurs (TV series), one of Earl Sinclair's favorite show is "Mister Ugh", a parody of Mister Ed featuring a caveman instead of a horse.

Episodes

Main article: List of Mister Ed episodes

DVD releases

MGM Home Entertainment released two *Best-of* collections of *Mister Ed* on DVD in Region 1. Volume 1 (released January 13, 2004) contains 21 episodes and Volume 2 (released March 8, 2005) contains 20 episodes. Due to poor sales, further volumes were not released.

MGM also released a single-disc release entitled *Mister Ed's Barnyard Favorites* on July 26, 2005 which contains the first eight episodes featured on Volume One.

Judging by the pattern of other CBS and Filmways programs of the era, it is possible that some episodes from the early seasons may have had their copyrights lapsed, and thus have fallen in the public domain. The Internet Archive (archive.org) has the episode entitled "Ed the Beneficiary" [1].

On June 18, 2009, Shout! Factory announced that they had acquired the rights to release *Mister Ed* on DVD. They have subsequently released the first three seasons on DVD in Region 1, as of June 1, 2010.

An early review of the 1st season DVD by Paul Mavis states that most of the episodes are the full-length versions; however eight of them are the edited versions.

DVD Name	Ep #	Release Date
Season One/The Complete First Season	26	October 6, 2009
The Complete Second Season	26	February 2, 2010
The Complete Third Season	26	June 1, 2010
The Complete Fourth Season	26	November 16, 2010
The Complete Fifth Season	26	TBA
The Complete Sixth Season	13	TBA

See also

Other films with talking horses include *Hot to Trot* (1988) and *Ready to Run* (2002). The names of the talking horses were Don and Thunder Jam (TJ) respectively.

External links

- *Mister Ed (original)* [2] at the Internet Movie Database
- *Mister Ed ep. "Ed the Beneficiary"* [1] available for free download at the Internet Archive [*more*]
- *Mister Ed (2004 remake)* [3] at the Internet Movie Database
- *Mister Ed* [4] at TV.com
- How did they get Mr. Ed to talk? [5] from the Straight Dope
- Mister Ed [6] at TV Acres
- Interview with Alan Young, October 17, 2007 [7]
- Archive of American Television interview with Alan Young [8]
- DVD review of Complete Season 1 and production history [9]

The Beverly Hillbillies

The Beverly Hillbillies	
b&w title screen	
Format	sitcom
Starring	Buddy Ebsen Irene Ryan Donna Douglas Max Baer Jr Raymond Bailey Nancy Kulp Bea Benaderet Harriet E. MacGibbon
Opening theme	The Ballad of Jed Clampett
Country of origin	United States
Language(s)	English
No. of seasons	9
No. of episodes	274 (List of episodes)
Production	
Executive producer(s)	Al Simon Martin Ransohoff
Location(s)	Bel-Air, Hollywood, Los Angeles, California
Running time	22–24 minutes
Broadcast	
Original channel	CBS
Picture format	black and white (1962–65) Color (1965–1971)
Audio format	monaural
Original run	September 26, 1962 – March 23, 1971
Status	Ended
Chronology	
Related shows	*The Beverly Hillbillies*

The Beverly Hillbillies

The Beverly Hillbillies is an American situation comedy originally broadcast for nine seasons on CBS from 1962 to 1971, starring Buddy Ebsen, Irene Ryan, Donna Douglas and Max Baer Jr

The series is about a poor backwoods family transplanted to Beverly Hills California after striking oil on their land. A Filmways production, it is the first in a genre of "fish out of water" themed television shows, and was followed in 1963 by country-cousin series *Petticoat Junction* and in 1965 by another country cousin, *Green Acres*.[citation needed]. The concept paved the way for later culture-conflict shows such as *McCloud*, *The Nanny*, *The Fresh Prince of Bel-Air*, and *Doc*. Panned by many entertainment critics of its time, it quickly became a huge ratings success for most of its nine-year run on CBS.

The Beverly Hillbillies ranked among the top twelve most watched series on television for seven of its nine seasons, twice ranking as the number one series of the year, with a number of episodes that remain among the most-watched television episodes of all time.

The ongoing popularity of the series spawned a 1993 film remake by 20th Century Fox.

Overview

The Beverly Hillbillies series starts with the OK Oil Company learning of an inadvertent strike in Jed Clampett's Tennessee swamp land. Patriarch Jed moves with his family into a mansion next door to his banker (Mr. Drysdale) in the wealthy Los Angeles County city of Beverly Hills, California, where he brings a moral, unsophisticated, and minimalistic lifestyle to the swanky, self-obsessed, and sometimes superficial community. The theme song introduces the viewer to the world's most fortunate hunting accident — whereby Jed shoots at game but instead hits "black gold". Lasting nine seasons and accumulating seven Emmy nominations, it remains in syndication on several cable stations including TV Land.

The Hillbillies themselves were Buddy Ebsen as the widowed patriarch Jed "J.D." Clampett; Irene Ryan as his ornery mother-in-law, Daisy May "Granny" Moses; Donna Douglas as his curvaceous, tom-boy daughter Elly May Clampett; and Max Baer Jr as Jethro, the brawny, half-witted son of his cousin Pearl Bodine. Pearl (played by Bea Benaderet) appeared in several episodes during the first season, as did Jethro's twin sister Jethrine, played by Baer in drag, using Linda Kaye Henning's voiceover. Pearl was the relative who prodded Jed to move to California, after being told his modest property could yield $25 million.

The supporting cast featured Raymond Bailey as Jed's greedy, unscrupulous banker Milburn Drysdale; Harriet E. MacGibbon as Drysdale's ostentatious wife Margaret Drysdale; and Nancy Kulp as "Miss" Jane Hathaway, Drysdale's scholarly, "plain-Jane" secretary, who pined for the clueless Jethro.

While Granny frequently mentioned that she was from Tennessee, the series never specified the state from which the Clampetts moved to California. However, they often referred to nearby towns such as Joplin, Branson, Springfield and Silver Dollar City, all of which are in southwest Missouri. In the eighth episode of season 8, named, "Manhattan Hillbillies", Granny tells the police officer in Central

Park that her family comes from Taney County (which is in southwest Missouri). Early episodes also contained several references to Eureka Springs, which is in northwest Arkansas. All of the communities are in the Ozark Mountains. The show's producer Paul Henning is from Independence, Missouri and donated 1534 acres (621 ha) for the Ruth and Paul Henning Conservation Area near Branson.

Animal trainer Frank Inn provided animals for all three of Hennings' hit shows, which included "Elly May's critters", such as chimp Alfie who portrayed Cousin Bessie, and Stretch, Jed's hunting bloodhound dog (known as Duke on the show).

A three-act stage play based on the pilot was written by David Rogers in 1968.

Theme music

The theme song "The Ballad of Jed Clampett" was written by producer and writer Paul Henning and originally performed by Bluegrass artists Flatt and Scruggs. The song was sung by Jerry Scoggins (backed by Flatt and Scruggs) over the opening and end credits of each episode. It was #44 on the music charts in 1962 and a #1 country hit. Flatt and Scruggs also had another Billboard country top ten hit with the comic "Pearl, Pearl, Pearl," an ode to the feminine charms of Miss Pearl Bodine who was featured in the episode "Jed Throws a Wingding," the first of several Flatt and Scruggs appearances on the show.

The six main cast members participated on a 1963 Columbia Records soundtrack album which featured original song numbers in character. Additionally, Ebsen, Ryan and Douglas each made a few solo recordings following the show's success, including Ryan's 1966 novelty single, "Granny's Miniskirt".

The series generally featured no country music beyond the bluegrass banjo theme song, although country star Roy Clark and the team of Flatt and Scruggs occasionally played on the program. Pop singer Pat Boone appeared on one episode as himself, with the premise that he hailed from the same area of the country as the Clampetts (Boone is, in fact, a native of Jacksonville, Florida although he spent most of his childhood in Tennessee).

The 1989 film "UHF" featured a "Weird Al" Yankovic parody music video, combining "The Ballad of Jed Clampett" and Dire Straits' "Money for Nothing".

Popularity

Written-off as lowbrow by some critics, the show shot to the top of the Nielsen ratings shortly after its premiere and stayed there for several seasons. During its first two seasons, it was the number one program in the U.S. During its second season, it earned some of the highest ratings ever recorded for a half-hour sitcom. The season two episode "The Giant Jackrabbit" also became the most watched telecast up to the time of its airing, and remains the most watched half-hour episode of a sitcom as well. The series enjoyed excellent ratings throughout its run, although it had fallen out of the top 20 most-watched shows during its final season.

The series received two Emmy nominations for Best Comedy Series (1963, 1964) as well as nominations for cast members Irene Ryan (twice nominated as Best Series Actress, 1963, 1964) and Nancy Kulp (nominated for Best Comedy Series Supporting Actress, 1966).

Nielsen ratings

- 1962–1963: #1
- 1963–1964: #1
- 1964–1965: #12
- 1965–1966: #8
- 1966–1967: #9
- 1967–1968: #12
- 1968–1969: #10
- 1969–1970: #18

Influence on other television shows

Because of the show's high ratings, CBS asked creator Paul Henning to pen two more folksy comedies, spawning a mini-genre of rural sitcoms during the 1960s. *Petticoat Junction* featured an extended family, including three pretty young women of marrying age, running a small hotel in the isolated rural town of Hooterville. *Green Acres* flipped the Clampetts' fish-out-of-water concept by depicting two city sophisticates moving to Hooterville, which was populated by oddball country bumpkins.

Certain actors appeared on more than one of these series:

- Bea Benaderet, who had played Jethro's mother during the first season of *The Beverly Hillbillies*, was the mother of the family on *Petticoat Junction*.
- Linda Kaye Henning, who provided the voiceover for the *Beverly Hillbillies* character Jethrine, portrayed Benaderet's daughter Betty Jo Bradley on *Petticoat Junction* (the only female who remained all seven seasons).
- Edgar Buchanan, who starred in all 222 episodes of *Petticoat Junction* and guest-starred in 17 episodes of *Green Acres,* also guested in three episodes of *The Beverly Hillbillies,* always as the character Uncle Joe Carson.
- Charles Lane played Homer Bedloe, vice president of the C. & F. W. Railroad, on both shows. He also played an apartment landlord to Jane Hathaway ("Foster Phinney") during the 1970–71 season.
- Sam Drucker, played by Frank Cady, of both *Petticoat Junction and Green Acres,* also appeared in several episodes of the *Beverly Hillbillies.*
- Several animal actors trained by Frank Inn, including Higgins the dog, also moved between series as needed.

Despite the actor cross-overs and the character Uncle Joe Carson's multiple appearances (which made it clear that the three shows were set in the same fictional universe), the two Hooterville series retained identities that were distinct from *The Beverly Hillbillies*.

Cancellation and "the Rural Purge"

Nielsen ratings for the 1970–71 season show that the bottom had dropped out for the perennial Top 30 series, but was still fairly popular when it was cancelled in 1971 after 274 episodes. The CBS network, prompted by pressure from advertisers seeking a more sophisticated urban audience, decided to refocus its schedule on several "hip" new urban-themed shows, and to make room for them, all of CBS's rural-themed comedies were simultaneously cancelled, despite some considerable Nielsen ratings. This action came to be known as "the Rural Purge". Pat Buttram, who played Mr Haney on *Green Acres*, famously remarked that, "It was the year CBS killed everything with a tree in it."

In addition to *The Beverly Hillbillies* (rated #18), the series that were eliminated included, *Green Acres*, *Mayberry R.F.D.* (rated #15), and *Hee Haw*, the last of which was resurrected in first-run syndication, where it ran for another twenty-one years. *Petticoat Junction* had been canceled a year earlier due to declining ratings following the death of its star, Bea Benaderet.

Main cast

Jedediah Clampett

> Although he had received little formal education, Jed Clampett had a good deal of common sense. A good-natured man, he is the apparent head of the family. Jed's wife (Elly May's mother) died, but is referred to in the episode "Duke Steals A Wife" as Rose Ellen. Jed was shown to be an expert marksman and was extremely loyal to his family and kinfolk. The huge oil pool in the swamp he owned was the beginning of his rags-to-riches journey to Beverly Hills. Although he longed for the old ways back in the hills, he made the best of being in Beverly Hills. Whenever he had anything on his mind, he would sit on the curbstone of his mansion and whittle until he came up with the answer. Jedediah, the version of Jed's name used in the 1993 *Beverly Hillbillies* theatrical movie, was never mentioned in the original television series (though coincidentally, on Ebsen's subsequent series, *Barnaby Jones*, Barnaby's nephew J.R. was also named Jedediah). In one episode Jed and Granny reminisce about seeing Buddy Ebsen and Vilma Ebsen—a joking reference to the Ebsens' song and dance act. Jed appears in all 274 episodes.

Granny (Daisy May Moses)

> Called "Granny" by all, relatives or not, shotgun-toting Daisy Moses, Jed's mother-in-law, is a true daughter of Dixie. Paul Henning, the show's creator/ producer quickly disposed of the idea of Granny being Jed's mother, which would have changed the show's dynamics, making Granny the matriarch and Jed subodinate to her. Granny could be aggressive, but often over-ruled by Jed. Granny is a revisionist reb to the core, defending President Jefferson Davis, the Stars and Bars, and the simple life. Short fused and easily angered, Granny fancies herself a "dunked" (not

"sprinkled") Christian with forgiveness in her heart. She abhors "revenuers" and blue-coat Yankees. A self-styled "M.D." — "mountain doctor" — she claims to have an edge over expensive know-nothing city physicians. In lieu of anesthesia, Granny uses her "white lightening" brew before commencing on such painful treatments such as leech bleeding and yanking teeth with pliers. Short and scrappy, she often wielded a double-barreled, 12-gauge shotgun. The lone time she shot it (with rock salt) was during a mock Indian invasion created by Mr. Drysdale. She was also able to tell the precise time via a sun dial, and the weather via a wooly caterpillar. Without her glasses, Granny was extremely nearsighted — once in a crossover with the Green Acres show, Granny mistook a dog for a baby child and a coffee pot for a telephone. Two of Granny's phobias were "Injuns" (she actually bought wigs so the Clampetts wouldn't be "scalped") and the "cement pond" (swimming pool–she has a fear of water). In a long story arc in the show's ninth season, Elly May dates a U.S. Navy frogman, which confuses Granny: After seeing the frogman climb out of the pool in his skin-diving wear, she thinks that anyone who swims in the pool will be turned into a frog. She also had a peculiar way of retelling the American Civil War, where she thought that the South had won, and Jefferson Davis was the President. Any attempts to correct her met with failure. She was also known for slicing off switches to use on Jethro mainly, whenever he went too far with his dumb and idiotic schemes.

There are references to Granny growing up in the Smoky Mountains of Tennessee. From episode 9: "When I was a girl back in Tennessee, I set so many boys' hearts on fire that they took to calling that neck of the woods *The Smoky Mountains*."

Granny's full name, Daisy Moses, allegedly a homage to the popular and dearly loved folk artist Anna Mary Robertson, known to the world as Grandma Moses. (Grandma Moses died in 1961, a year before *The Beverly Hillbillies* made its television debut.) Granny is frequently referred to as "Granny Clampett" in a number of episodes but technically she was a Moses. Granny appears in all 274 episodes.

Elly May Clampett

Elly May, Jed's only child, is a mountain beauty with the body of a pinup girl and the soul of a tomboy. She could throw a fastball as well as "rassle" most men to a fall. She could be as tender with her friends, animals and people, as she was tough with Jethro or anyone else she was rasslin'. She said once that animals could be better companions than people, but as she grew older she saw that, "fellas kin be more fun than critters." Elly was squired about by eager young Hollywood actors with stage names like "Dash Riprock" and "Bolt Upright". Other boyfriends for Elly included Sonny Drysdale, Beau Short, beatnik Sheldon Epps and Mark Templeton, a frogman.

Elly's most notable weakness, oft mentioned when she was being "courted", was her lack of kitchen skills. Family members would cringe when, for plot reasons, Elly would take over the kitchen. Rock-like donuts and cookies, for example, were a plot function in an episode featuring

Wally Cox as bird watching Professor Biddle.

Elly is briefly considered for film stardom at the movie studio owned by Jed. In one episode, hearing Rock Hudson and Cary Grant are both single, Granny asks that Elly be introduced to them.

During the final season's episodes, Elly May takes a job as a secretary at the Commerce Bank this is the end result of the secretaries of the bank taking offense to Mr. Drysdale's treatment of them. they got Elly May to agree to the job because her father and granny thought it would be a good way for her to "meet a husband". Miss Jane knew he would not mistreat the employees in front of the Clampettes. Mr. Drysdale not being able to mistreat the secretarial pool by forcing them to work off the clock,and other abuses. since the clampetts only had their money in the bank because of their erroneous belief that Mr. Drysdale was a kind and generous man.

In the 1981 TV movie of *The Beverly Hillbillies*, Elly May is head of a zoo. Elly May appears in all 274 episodes.

Jethro Bodine

Jethro is the son of Jed's cousin, Pearl Bodine. He drove the Clampett family to their new home in California and stayed on with them to further his education. The whole family boasted of Jethro's "sixth grade education" but nevertheless felt he was a bit of an idiot. Jethro was simply naive in the first season of the show, but became incredibly ignorant and pompous as the series progressed. He often showed off his cyphering abilities with multiplication and "go-zin-ta's", as in "five gozinta five one times, five gozinta ten two times," etc. After that, he decided to go to college. He managed to enroll late in the semester at a local secretarial school due to his financial backing and earned his diploma by the end of the day because he didn't understand what was going on in class and was too disruptive. (This was an in-joke—in real life Max Baer Jr, has a Masters degree).

Many stories in the series involved Jethro's endless career search, which included such diverse vocations as brain surgeon, street car conductor, double-naught spy, Hollywood producer (a studio flunky remarks Jethro has the *right qualifications* for being a producer-a 6th grade education and his uncle owns the studio. The in-joke gag of Jethro as a movie producer was replayed in the 1981 movie), soda jerk, short order cook, and once as a bookkeeper for Milburn Drysdale's bank. More often than not, his overall goal in these endeavors was to obtain as many pretty girls as humanly possible, which were usually the catalyst that prompted him to do so. While working as a producer, Jethro called himself "Beef Jerky", a wannabe playboy and man-about-town sophisticate. Out of all the Clampett clan, he was the one who made the most changes from 'country bumpkin' to 'city boy.' Another running gag is that Jethro was known as the "six foot stomach" for his ability to eat: in one episode he ate a jetliner's entire supply of steaks; in another episode Jethro tried to set himself up as a Hollywood agent for cousin "Bessie"-with a fee of 10,000 bananas for Bessie and 1,000 bananas for Jethro. Jed once mentioned that Jethro was the only baby he knew born with a full set of teeth "just like a beaver". Jethro could never succeed in any career he tried. Jethro appears in 273 episodes; he is not in the second-to-last episode but Baer of course remains billed in the title credits. Baer claimed he only auditioned for the role of Jethro for fun, and never expected to get the part. Supposedly, he clinched the part largely because of his grin.

Duke

The Clampetts' family dog. He's an old bloodhound that Jed had bought for four bits (50 cents) when he was a puppy. In early episodes, Jethro tried to teach Duke to fetch sticks, though to Jed, it looked as if Duke taught Jethro how to do that trick. In a couple of episodes, Duke got involved with a French poodle that was brought in to mate with Mrs. Drysdale's pampered pooch Claude. Apparently, the poodle had better taste and had Duke's puppies instead. When Mrs. Drysdale wanted Claude to get revenge against Duke, Jed warned her that he'd seen that old hound dog hold his own against a bobcat.

The Drysdales

Milburn, Margaret and Sonny: The Drysdales are the Clampetts' next door neighbors. Milburn is the Commerce Bank's tightwad President and the friendly bumpkins' confidant. The haughty Mrs. Drysdale touted a heritage that traced back to the Mayflower, but money-hungry Milburn's concerns were strictly monetary. When suffering an anxiety attack, Milburn sniffs a stack of money and is quickly revived. Although wife Margaret, a blue-blooded Bostonian, had obvious disdain for the "peasant" hillbillies, she tacitly agrees to tolerate them (rather than Milburn lose their ever growing account- which was $96,000,000 in 1969, equal to $569704918 today). Margaret loathed all four "vagabonds", but her most heated rivalry was with Granny, with whom she occasionally had some "scraps". Ray Bailey appears in 247 episodes. Harriet MacGibbon appears in 55 episodes between 1962 and 1969, she is not seen in the last two seasons of the show although is occasionally mentioned. Margaret's aged father had gambled away most of their money. Mrs. Drysdale's son Sonny, was a thirty-something collegian who didn't believe in working-up a sweat. Sonny Drysdale was Milburn Drysdale's stepson (played by Louis Nye), and an insufferable mama's boy. Finding Elly-May a lovely, naive, Pollyanna, he courted her until she literally tossed him. Although the character was fondly remembered by fans, Sonny only appeared in four episodes, three in 1962 and a final appearance in 1966. Mr. Drysdale appeased the Clampetts and said that anything they did was unquestionably right. He often forced others, especially his secretary, to placate to the Clampetts' unorthodox requests.

Jane Hathaway

Jane Hathaway, whom the Clampetts addressed as "Miss Jane," is Drysdale's loyal and efficient secretarial assistant. Though she always carried out his wishes, she was inherently decent and was frequently put off by her boss' greed. When she was annoyed with him, as was often especially when one of Drysdale's schemes went too far, she would usually and forcefully say

"Chief!" Unlike Drysdale (who was merely interested in the Clampetts' wealth), Jane was genuinely fond of them (to the Clampetts, she was considered family; even Granny, the one most dead-set against living in California, liked her very much and thought of her as part of the family), in fact, she actually harbored something of a crush on Jethro for most of the series' run. At first, she mistook the Clampetts as the servants, until she realized who they really were (which almost cost her her job). Miss Hathaway frequently has to "rescue" Drysdale from his idiotic schemes, receiving little or no thanks for her efforts. In one episode, she and Granny, disguised as "geisha girls," finally have enough and "crown" Drysdale and Jethro, who have made one too many comments about women serving men. Jane is loyal to Drysdale as well, despite her misgivings toward his avarice and greed. In one episode, the Clampetts, feeling money has corrupted them, give all of their money to Virginia "Ginny" Jennings (Sheila Kuehl), a college student. While Drysdale moans the loss of the money, Jane immediately tells him to stop thinking about the Clampetts and start trying to get the Jennings account. Eventually, everyone discovered Jennings' real motives, and she was gone, with the Clampetts getting their money back, and things were as they were before. In one episode, it is established that Miss Jane sacrificed her job as the top secretary of the top executive of the top insurance company to join Mr. Drysdale at the Commerce Bank. Miss Jane was a Vassar graduate. Jane Hathaway appears in 246 episodes.

Semi-regulars

Pearl

Jed's cousin Pearl Bodine—portrayed by Bea Benaderet—was Jethro's mother. She was a generally well-meaning mother to Jethro. She also was a popular character, often used as a foil for Granny, and became a regular part way through the first season (the end credits were even refilmed to include Pearl with the other family members). She disappeared after the first year because Benaderet had become the star of another Paul Henning series, *Petticoat Junction*. Like Elly May, Pearl's name came from that of a character (Pearl Lester) in the popular rural-life novel, play, and film *Tobacco Road*. Pearl Bodine appears in 22 of the first season's episodes, 1962–63, and later makes a cameo in the 1967 episode "Greetings From The President". In the Episodes "The Clampetts Get Psychoanalyzed" & "The Psychiatrist Gets Clampetted" Herbert Rudley plays the psychiatrist Dr. Eugene Twombley. In the episodes Pearl is enamored with Dr. Twombley; Benaderet's real life husband is named Eugene Twombley. The role was first offered to Shirley Collie.

Jetherine Bodine

Jetherine is Pearl's king-sized daughter, Jethro's twin (and is also played by Baer, though voice by Linda Kaye). Jetherine appears in 11 episodes in 1962–63; she moves with her mother to the Clampett mansion later that season but occasionally is not seen in episodes during her stay in

California. Jetherine was upset in leaving the hills as it meant separation from her "sweetie", traveling salesman Jazzbo Depew. Late in the season it was explained in an episode that Jetherine had returned home to marry Depew, although the wedding was never seen in the series (nor was Jetherine ever seen again, although she was occasionally referenced). Jethro and Jetherine rarely appeared in the same scene in any of the programs and then they were never on-camera at the same time except for the rare back-of-the-head shot of one done by a double. Jetherine appears in the 1993 movie version.

Dash Riprock

Dash played by Larry Pennell was the handsome Hollywood actor employed by Jed's movie studio. He and Ellie May met while she was working as an extra at the studio. Once Dash saw the beautiful Elly in her bathing suit, he was smitten with her. The two had an on-and-off relationship. In one episode, Mr. Drysdale forced Dash into courting Elly May by threatening to put him in a television show called *Crabman*. Elly initially liked Dash and enjoyed being with him on dates. Jethro, however, was more enamored with Dash and his playboy persona than was his comely cousin. Riprock was a send-up of the blatantly fake screen names employed by a number of movie actor's of the period. Riprock's real name (before being changed by Hollywood moguls) was "Homer Noodleman," and he was from Peoria, Illinois. Dash Riprock was in 10 episodes, mainly between 1965–69.

Lowell Redlings Farquhar

Lowell is the elderly father of Mrs. Drysdale whom Granny considers a potential beau. Lowell (played by Charles Ruggles) is in three episodes, 1965–66.

Lester Flatt and Earl Scruggs

Country music stars Flatt and Scruggs play themselves in seven episodes, 1963–68, who are longtime friends of the Clampetts "back home" (Kimberling City, Missouri) who visit with the Clampetts when they are on tour in California. The duo had a number-one Billboard country single with the show's "The Ballad of Jed Clampett" (although the song is actually performed in the credits by Jerry Scroggins to Flatt and Scruggs' instrumental). Actress Joi Lansing plays Flatt's wife, Gladys, in five episodes, 1963–68.

John Brewster

Brewster (played by Frank Wilcox), is the oil tycoon who purchases the oil rights to the gusher on the Clampett home back in the hills. The Clampetts are quite fond of him, and his wife occasionally visits them in California. John Brewster appears in 14 episodes, 1962–1966.

Janet Trego

Janet (played by Sharon Tate) is a beautiful secretary at the Commerce Bank. Although Janet appears in 15 episodes, 1963–65, her role is generally quite minor. Tate was later murdered by Charles Manson's "Family" just before the start of the eighth season.

Sam Drucker

Sam (played by Frank Cady) owns the general store in Hooterville. Granny is constantly under the impression that Sam wants to marry her, however Sam has no intentions of doing so. He appears in 10 episodes between 1968–1970. Cady also starred as Sam Drucker in 31 episodes of the television series *Petticoat Junction* and in 142 episodes in the series *Green Acres*. Cady reprised the role of Sam Drucker for the 1990 *Green Acres* reunion movie *Return to Green Acres*

Helen Thompson

Helen (played by Danielle Mardi) is a beautiful British secretary at the Commerce Bank. Helen takes over Jane Hathaway's job as Mr. Drysdale's secretary after Ms. Hathaway resigned. Helen appears in 17 episodes between 1969–1971. Helen was one of the ringleaders of the protest group the secretaries of the Commerce Bank created, GRUN (Girls Resist Unfair Neglect). She, along with many other secretaries as well as Elly and Granny, lived with Ms. Hathaway for a short time in her apartment.

Shorty Kellums

Shorty (played by Shug Fisher) is Jed's longtime buddy from back home whom Jed reunites with in 1969 when the Clampetts go back for an extended period to the Hills. Shorty is a wiry little man who is crazy about voluptuous girls half his age. Shorty later moves into the Clampett mansion in Beverly Hills for a period. Shorty Kellums appears in 17 episodes in the 1969–70 season, and returned again briefly during 1970–71.

Elverna Bradshaw

Elverna is Granny's longtime rival back in the Hills, a gossip second to none. She makes a brief appearance in a 1963 episode when the Clampetts go back to the Hills to fetch Pearl to California but is not seen again until 1969 when the Clampetts return to their native land for an extended visit. However, both Granny and Jed referred to the character in several episodes throughout the series' run. Elverna (played by Elvia Allman) and Granny rekindle their feud in a match to see who will be first wed, Elverna's daughter or Elly May. For reasons not really explained, Elverna also moves into the Clampett Beverly Hills mansion during the same period that Shorty does, both of them however are gone from the estate for the final 1970–71 season, presumably having returned back home. {A running gag was Shorty literally running to keep from being married to Elverna and Jed Clampet having to catch Shorty}. Elverna Bradshaw appears in 13 episodes, 1963–1970.

Matthew Templeton/Mark Templeton

The Templetons are two brothers both played by actor Roger Torrey. Matthew is seen in three episodes in October 1969 during the Clampetts stay in the Hills where Granny tags the preacherman as a prospective husband for Elly. Unfortunately, Granny learns that Matthew is married. Just a year later back in California, Elly meets Matthew's brother, Mark Templeton, who is a marine biologist, a frogman whom Granny believes is actually part frog. The Mark Templeton storyline is considered by many Hillbillies fans as the best of the series and played out for nine popular episodes and was abruptly dropped although advance publicity for the show indicated Elly May and Mark would be marrying during the season. It was cancelled at the end of the season despite fairly good ratings. Roger Torrey auditioned for the part of Jethro, and many believe he would have gotten the part had Max Baer not auditioned for it.

The "critters"

In addition to the family dog, Duke, a number of animals lived on the Clampett estate thanks to animal-lover Elly. These animals were collectively known as her "critters".

The most prominent pets were chimpanzees. The first chimp on the show was named "Skipper", who was a Christmas present from Mr. Drysdale. The following season, Elly May acquired a female chimp named "Cousin Bessie", so named because she was Skipper's cousin. She was a regular for the remainder of the series. A running gag is that Cousin Bessie frequently proves to be smarter than "educated" Jethro. There was also a chimp called Maybelle.

As well as typical pets such as dogs/puppies and cats/kittens Elly was also shown to keep exotic animals such as deer, possums, a bear named Fairchild, some goats, a raccoon named Elmer, a kangaroo, Earl the rooster, Charlie the skunk, Gem the mink, a puma named Jethro, a hippo named Harold, a sea lion named Shorty and many more. There was also a mutt named Jojo and a wild pig named Pearl.

The trainer of all the animals in the series was Frank Inn, who also trained the animals for the contemporaneous rural comedy series *Petticoat Junction* and *Green Acres*.

Series storylines

Most episodes revolved around the clash between the "uncivilized" hillbilly culture represented by the Clampetts and the "civilized" American culture of the Drysdales. The Clampetts lived as they always had, even in their large, elegant mansion, never abandoning their mountain attire or replacing the old rattletrap truck in which they had moved to California. Although when asked what kind of truck it is, Jethro said 'I think it's a Stutz', it is actually based on a 1922 Oldsmobile. All the Hillbillies were handy with firearms and always seemed to have their weapons close at hand and ready to draw. They continued to grow their own food, and Granny made lye soap and moonshine. The extreme potency of the moonshine liquor and the harshness of the lye soap were running gags throughout the run of the series.

As another running joke, the movie theaters back in the hills were still showing films from the silent movie era and the Hillbillies were unaware of talking pictures or more contemporary movie stars. Granny's favorite actor was Hoot Gibson, but she also had an intense crush on William S. Hart, and the whole Clampett family adored Mary Pickford. Silent movie legend Gloria Swanson made a memorable guest appearance on the show as herself in an episode that featured a comic parody of a silent melodrama. The Clampetts did, however, have a television, on which they watched soap operas and "rasslin'", as well as John Wayne movies, as he was apparently one of the few "talkie" movie stars of whom they were aware. Wayne made a brief cameo as himself after the Clampett mansion was "attacked" by stuntmen dressed as Native Americans.

Pearl and Granny often fought for kitchen supremacy. Pearl once told Granny "a blood cousin trumps a mother-in-law". This underscored a familial disconnect between Jethro and Granny; although they shared no bloodlines, Jethro still called her "Granny" (as did everyone else on the show, including Jane and the Drysdales). Other than their kitchen wars, relations between Granny and Pearl were generally friendly. The second season began with a brief mention of Pearl having moved back to the hills, an ironic departure, as it was Pearl who had urged Jed to move to California. The change came about because actress Bea Benaderet had left the show to star in *Petticoat Junction*). Mrs. Drysdale soon became Granny's main sparring partner.

Although both Douglas and Baer were well into their twenties when the series started, during the first years of the series, their characters were supposed to be teenagers. Elly May was enrolled in an elite girls' school in the first season, although no further mention was made of her education in later episodes. Jethro was enrolled in a sixth-grade class with much younger students; a few episodes later on, the scripts suggested that he was still in school.

A running theme during the series involved the outlandish efforts Mr. Drysdale took to keep the Clampetts in Beverly Hills (and their money in his bank). Their desires to return to the mountains were often prompted by Granny after some perceived slight she received from the "city-folk" around them. Drysdale went so far as to re-create the log cabin the Clampetts had lived in and place it right next to the "cee-ment pond" and the still Granny had installed to make moonshine. Another time Drysdale followed the Clampetts to the "Hills" and bought up the Silver Dollar City "bank" just to make sure he had a controlling interest in the Clampetts' money. One running gag was that when Jed would take money out of his pocket, Drysdale's blood pressure would go up. A similar running joke was that when it seemed the Clampetts would take their money out of his bank, Drysdale's face would turn green. A variation of the joke of Drysdale's face changing color is in one episode when, after being given some of Granny's "Tennessee Tranquilizer" (moonshine), Drysdale's face turns red.

Another frequent source of humor dealt with Jethro's endless career search, which included such diverse vocations as soda jerk, brain surgeon, Hollywood celebrity, and secret "double naught" agent/spy. Jethro coveted movie star fame and relished becoming a "playboy" like Elly's beau Dash Riprock. Jethro's stupidity usually caused such career attempts to fail spectacularly, as when he decided to open a "topless" restaurant ("The Happy Gizzard"), where the waiters and waitresses were hatless. The one time in the series when Jethro almost succeeded as a "Hollywood celebrity" was when "Cousin Roy" (Roy Clark) tried to get Jethro to back him up as a country singer in Hollywood; Jethro refused and failed as usual. Jethro did have one success, of sorts. When he rescued a Bird Watchers girl troop who fell into the "cement pond" (they were attacked by ants), Jethro got a "lifesaving badge"!

Misunderstandings were a general source of humor in the program: when the Clampetts did not understand something they had never encountered before (such as a water faucet), or when various city dwellers could not comprehend something the Clampetts were talking about. A group of businessmen overheard Jed talking about "crawdads" and concluded that he was discussing a new type of military vehicle, which they wanted to invest in.

The Clampetts went back to the hills for Christmas during the first season but did not return there until the eighth season, during which several episodes were filmed on location in Kimberling City, Missouri. During this period, Shug Fisher and Elvia Allman joined the cast as Shorty and Elverna (Allman had appeared on an episode in the first season playing the same character).

One constant throughout the series was that the Hillbillies, who were scrupulously honest, were surrounded by cynical, conniving and money-hungry "city-folk," whose plans were always foiled (usually unknowingly) by the Clampetts.

Merchandise

The 1960s saw a plethora of tie-in merchandise hit store shelves, particularly toys. Several different coloring books and jigsaw puzzles were released, as was a fairly long-running comic book. There were even Hillbillies Halloween costumes. A *Beverly Hillbillies* lunchbox is among the most valuable pieces of memorabilia from the era.

The Beverly Hillbillies made the cover of *TV Guide* nine times between 1962 and 1970. Donna Douglas is the only cast member pictured on every cover. Donna Douglas was also one of the most publicized actresses of the era, making the covers of many movie magazines.

In 1993, a 110-card set of *Beverly Hillbillies* trading cards was released by Eclipse Comics. Although timed to coincide with the release of the 1993 *Beverly Hillbillies* film, these cards featured photos from the original television series, with storylines and character details on the back. An earlier card series from 1963 is highly sought by collectors and is among the most expensive non-sports cards sets.

Reunions

1981 CBS TV movie

In 1981, a *Return of the Beverly Hillbillies* television movie, written and produced by series creator Paul Henning, was aired on the CBS network. Irene Ryan had died in 1973, and Raymond Bailey had died in 1980. The script acknowledged Granny's passing but featured Imogene Coca as Granny's mother. Max Baer decided against reprising the role that both started and stymied his career, so the character of Jethro Bodine was given to another actor, Ray Young.

The film's plot had Jed back in his old homestead in Bugtussle, having divided his massive fortune among Elly May and Jethro, both of whom stayed on the West Coast. Jane Hathaway had become a Department of Energy agent and was seeking Granny's "White Lightnin'" recipe to combat the energy crisis. Since Granny had gone on to "her re-ward", it was up to Granny's centenarian "Maw" (Imogene Coca) to divulge the secret brew's ingredients. Subplots included Jethro playing an egocentric, starlet-starved Hollywood producer, Jane and her boss (Werner Klemperer) having a romance and Elly May owning a large petting zoo. The four main characters finally got together by the end of the story.

Having been filmed a mere decade after the final episode of the original series, viewer consensus was that the series' original spirit was lost to the film on many fronts, chief of which being the deaths of Ryan and Bailey and Baer's absence, which left only three of the six original cast members available to reprise their respective roles. Further subtracting from the familiarity was the fact that the legendary Clampett mansion was unavailable for a location shoot as the owners' lease was too expensive. Henning himself admitted sheer embarrassment when the finished product aired, blaming his inability to rewrite the script due to the 1981 Writers Guild strike.

The Last Hillbilly Hurrah

In 1993, Ebsen, Douglas, and Baer reunited onscreen for the only time in the CBS-TV retrospective television special, *The Legend of the Beverly Hillbillies* which ranked as the 4th most watched television program of the week — a major surprise given the mediocre rating for the 1981 TV-movie. It was a rare tribute from the "Tiffany network" which owed much of its success in the 1960s to the series but has often seemed embarrassed by it in hindsight, often down-playing the show in retrospective television specials on the network's history and rarely inviting cast members to participate in such all-star broadcasts.

The Legend of The Beverly Hillbillies special ignored several plot twists of the TV movie, notably Jethro was now not a film director but a leading Los Angeles physician. Critter-loving Elly May was still in California with her animals but Jed was back home in the Hills, having lost his fortune, stolen by the now-imprisoned banker Drysdale (a plot twist that many fans found unsettling for this good-natured show.) Nancy Kulp had died in 1991 and was little referred to beyond the multitude of film clips that dotted the special (which curiously failed to include a single film clip of Harriet MacGibbon.) The special was released on VHS tape by CBS/Fox Video in 1995 and as a bonus feature on The Official Third Season DVD Set in 2009.

Reruns and syndication

The Beverly Hillbillies is still televised daily around the world in syndication. In the United States, the show is broadcast on TV Land and WGN America. A limited number of episodes from the earlier portions of the series run have turned up in the public domain and as such are seen occasionally on many smaller networks.

The show is distributed by CBS Television Distribution, the syndication arm of CBS Paramount Television. The repeats of the show that debuted on CBS Daytime on September 5–9, 1966 as "Mornin' Beverly Hillbillies" through September 10, 1971 and on September 13–17, 1971 as "The Beverly HILLBILLIES" lasted up to Winter 1971–1972. It aired at 11:00–11:30am Eastern/10:00-10:30am Central through September 3, 1971, then moved to 10:30–11:00am Eastern/9:30-10:00am Central for the last season on CBS Daytime.

Media

VHS and DVD releases

Many episodes of the first two seasons of the series are in the public domain because CBS, having bought the rights to the series shortly after its cancellation, neglected to renew their copyrights. As a result, these episodes have been unofficially released on home video and DVD on many low-budget labels and shown on low-power television stations and low-budget networks in 16 mm prints. In many video prints of the public domain episodes, the original and much-loved theme music has been replaced by generic music due to copyright issues.

However, before his death, Paul Henning, whose estate now holds the original film elements to the public domain episodes, authorized MPI Home Video to officially release the best of the first two seasons on DVD, the first "ultimate collection" of which was released in the fall of 2005. These collections include the original, uncut versions of the first season's episodes, complete with their original theme music and opening sponsor plugs. Vol. 1 has, among its bonus features, the alternate, un-aired version of the pilot film, *The Hillbillies Of Beverly Hills* (the version of the episode that sold the series to CBS), and the "cast commercials" (cast members pitching the products of the show's sponsors) originally shown at the end of each episode.

For many years, 20th Century Fox, through a joint venture with CBS called CBS/Fox Video, officially released select episodes of *Hillbillies* on videocassette. After Viacom merged with CBS, Paramount Home Entertainment (the video division of Paramount Pictures, which was acquired by Viacom in 1994) took over the video rights.

In 2006, Paramount announced plans to release the copyrighted episodes in boxed sets through CBS DVD later that year. The show's second season (consisting of the public domain episodes from that season) was released on DVD in Region 1 on October 7, 2008 as "...The Official Second Season". The third season was released on February 17, 2009. Both seasons are available to be purchased together from major online retailers.

See also

- List of The Beverly Hillbillies episodes
- *The Beverly Hillbillies* (1993), a movie based on the series
- "Money For Nothing/Beverly Hillbillies", a song by "Weird Al" Yankovic
- Zeke Manners, who led a band called The Beverly Hillbillies in the 1930s
- Rural purge

External links

- *The Beverly Hillbillies* [1] at the Internet Movie Database
- *The Beverly Hillbillies* [2] at TV.com
- Watch full episodes of *The Beverly Hillbillies* [3] on TVLand.com
- *The Beverly Hillbillies* [4] at the Museum of Broadcast Communications
- Beverly Hillbillies Theme Bluegrass Lyrics (The Ballad of Jed Clampett) [5]

The Man from U.N.C.L.E.

The Man from U.N.C.L.E.	
Genre	Spy-fi
Format	Espionage
Developed by	Sam Rolfe
Starring	Robert Vaughn David McCallum Leo G. Carroll
Theme music composer	Jerry Goldsmith
Country of origin	United States
No. of seasons	4
No. of episodes	105 (List of episodes)
Production	
Executive producer(s)	Norman Felton
Camera setup	Single-camera
Running time	50 min.
Broadcast	
Original channel	NBC
Picture format	Black-and-white (1964–1965) Color (1965–1968) 4:3
Audio format	Monaural
Original run	September 22, 1964 – January 15, 1968
Status	Ended
Chronology	
Related shows	*The Girl from U.N.C.L.E.*

The Man from U.N.C.L.E. is an American television series that was broadcast on NBC from September 22, 1964, to January 15, 1968. It follows the exploits of two secret agents, played by Robert Vaughn and David McCallum, who work for a fictitious secret international law-enforcement agency called U.N.C.L.E. (the United Network Command for Law and Enforcement).

Background

105 episodes were produced between 1964 and 1968. The series was created by Metro-Goldwyn-Mayer. The first season was broadcast in black-and-white.

James Bond creator Ian Fleming contributed to the show's creation. The book *The James Bond Films* reveals that Fleming's TV concept had two characters: Napoleon Solo and April Dancer (*The Girl from U.N.C.L.E.*). ("Mr. Solo" was originally the name of a crime boss in Fleming's *Goldfinger*.) Robert Towne and Harlan Ellison wrote scripts for the series, which was originally to have been titled *Solo*. Author Michael Avallone, who wrote the first original novel based upon the series (see below), is sometimes incorrectly cited as the creator of the series (such as in the January 1967 issue of *The Saint Magazine*). At one point, Fleming's name was to have been connected more directly with the series. The cover of the original prospectus for the series showed the title *Ian Fleming's Solo*. Solo was originally slated to be the "solo" star of the series, the only "Man". But a small scene by a Russian agent named Illya Kuryakin caught fire with the fans, and the two were permanently paired.

Premise

The series centered on a two-man troubleshooting team working for U.N.C.L.E.: American Napoleon Solo (Robert Vaughn), and Russian Illya Kuryakin (David McCallum). Leo G. Carroll played Alexander Waverly, the British head of the organization (Number One of Section One). Lisa Rogers (Barbara Moore) joined the cast as a female regular in the fourth season.

The series, though fictional, achieved such notability as to have artifacts (props, costumes and documents, and a video clip) from the show included in the Ronald Reagan Presidential Library's exhibit on spies and counterspies. Similar exhibits can be found in the museums of the Central Intelligence Agency and other agencies and organizations involved with intelligence gathering.

U.N.C.L.E.'s archenemy was a vast organization known as THRUSH (originally named WASP in the series pilot movie). The original series never explained what the acronym THRUSH stood for, but in several of the U.N.C.L.E. novels written by David McDaniel, it was expanded as the **T**echnological **H**ierarchy for the **R**emoval of **U**ndesirables and the **S**ubjugation of **H**umanity, and described by him as having been founded by Col. Sebastian Moran after the death of Professor Moriarty at the Reichenbach Falls in the Sherlock Holmes story "The Final Problem". Later, an alternate—and more plausible—explanation was offered, with THRUSH rising out of the fall of Nazism and founded by high-ranking Nazi officials—including Martin Bormann—who fled to Argentina when defeat was seen as inevitable, taking with them enormous financial wealth, including gold and precious works of art.

THRUSH's aim was to conquer the world. Napoleon Solo said (in "The Green Opal Affair"), "THRUSH believes in the two-party system: the masters and the slaves", adding in another episode ("The Vulcan Affair") that THRUSH will "kill people the way people kill flies: a careless flick of the wrist -- reflex action." So dangerous was the threat from THRUSH that governments, even those most ideologically opposed such as the United States and the USSR, cooperated in the formation and operation of U.N.C.L.E. Similarly, if Solo and Kuryakin held opposing political views, the writers allowed little to show in their interactions.

Though executive producer Norman Felton and Ian Fleming had developed the character of Napoleon Solo, it was producer Sam Rolfe who created the organization of U.N.C.L.E. Unlike the nationalistic organizations of the CIA and James Bond's MI6, U.N.C.L.E. was a worldwide organization composed of agents from all corners of the globe. The character of Illya Kuryakin was created by Rolfe as a Russian U.N.C.L.E. agent.

The creators of the series decided that the involvement of an innocent character would be part of each episode, giving the audience someone with whom it could identify. Through all the changes in series in the course of four seasons, this element remained a factor—from a suburban housewife in the pilot, "The Vulcan Affair" (film version: "To Trap a Spy"), to the various people kidnapped in the final episode, "The Seven Wonders of the World Affair".

The Organization

Main article: U.N.C.L.E.

Season 1

The show's first season was in black and white. Rolfe created a kind of Alice in Wonderland world, where mundane everyday life would intermittently intersect with the looking-glass fantasy of international espionage which lay just beyond. The U.N.C.L.E. universe was one where the weekly "innocent" would get caught up in a series of fantastic adventures, in a battle of good and evil. In its idealistic depiction of an international organization that transcended borders and agents of all nationalities worked together, Rolfe's U.N.C.L.E. anticipated Gene Roddenberry's interstellar United Federation of Planets in *"Star Trek"* two seasons later. Rolfe also blended deadly suspense with a light touch, reminiscent of Hitchcock. In fact, *U.N.C.L.E.* owes just as much to Alfred Hitchcock as it does to Ian Fleming, the touchstone being *North by Northwest*, where an innocent man is mistaken for an agent of a top secret organization, one of whose top members is played by Leo G. Carroll. This role led to Carroll being cast as Mr. Waverly in the show.

U.N.C.L.E. headquarters in New York City was most frequently entered by a secret entrance in Del Floria's Tailor Shop. Another entrance was through The Masque Club. Mr. Waverly had his own secret entrance. Unlike the competing TV series *I Spy* however, the shows were overwhelmingly shot on the MGM back lot. The same outside staircase was used for episodes set throughout the Mediterranean and Latin America, and the same eucalyptus dirt road on the back lot in Culver City stood in for virtually every continent of the globe. The episodes followed a naming convention where each title was in the form of "The ***** Affair", such as "The Vulcan Affair", "The Mad, Mad, Tea Party Affair", "The Waverly Ring Affair", and "The Deadly Quest Affair", the only exceptions being, "Alexander the

Greater Affair", parts 1 & 2. The first season episode "The Green Opal Affair" establishes that U.N.C.L.E. itself uses the term "Affair" to refer to its different missions.

Rolfe endeavored to make the implausibility of it all seem not only feasible but entertaining. Frogmen emerging from wells in Iowa, shootouts between U.N.C.L.E. and THRUSH agents in a crowded midtown Manhattan movie theater, top secret organizations hidden behind innocuous brownstone facades—this was a parallel universe that lay just beyond our own. Wikipedia:Neutral point of view#

The series also began to dabble in science fiction-based plots, beginning with "The Double Affair" in which a THRUSH agent, made to look like Solo through plastic surgery, infiltrates a secret U.N.C.L.E. facility where an immensely powerful weapon called "Project Earthsave" is stored; according to the dialogue, the weapon was developed to protect against a potential alien threat to Earth.

Rolfe left the show at the conclusion of the first season.

In its first season *The Man from U.N.C.L.E.* competed against *The Red Skelton Show* on CBS and Walter Brennan's short-lived *The Tycoon* on ABC.

Seasons 2–4

Switching to color, *U.N.C.L.E.* continued to enjoy huge popularity, but the new producer, David Victor, read articles that called the show a spoof and that is what it became. Over the next three seasons, five different show runners would supervise the *U.N.C.L.E.* franchise, and each one took the show in a direction that differed considerably from that of the first season. Furthermore, *U.N.C.L.E.* had spawned a swarm of imitators. In 1964, it was the only American spy show on U.S. TV; by 1966, there were nearly a dozen. In an attempt to emulate the success of ABC's mid-season hit, *Batman*, which had proven hugely popular on its debut in spring of 1966, *U.N.C.L.E.* moved swiftly towards self-parody and slapstick.

This campiness was most in evidence during the third season, when the producers made a conscious decision to increase the level of humor (though season two had moved in this direction in episodes such as "The Yukon Affair" and "The Indian Affairs Affair"). With episodes like "The My Friend the Gorilla Affair" (which featured a scene in which Solo is shown dancing with a gorilla) the show tested the loyalties of its supporters and this new direction resulted in a severe ratings drop, and nearly resulted in the show's cancellation. It was renewed for a fourth season and an attempt was made to go back to serious storytelling, but the ratings never recovered and *U.N.C.L.E.* was cancelled midway through the season.

Episodes

Main article: List of The Man from U.N.C.L.E. episodes

Theme music

The theme music, written by Jerry Goldsmith, changed slightly each season. Goldsmith only provided three original scores and was replaced by Morton Stevens, who composed four scores for the series. After Stevens, Walter Scharf did six scores, and Lalo Schifrin (who later wrote the *Mission: Impossible* theme) did two. Gerald Fried was composer from season two through the beginning of season four. The final composers were Robert Drasnin, Nelson Riddle and Richard Shores. The music reflected the show's changing seasons – Goldsmith, Stevens and Scharf composed dramatic scores in the first season using brass, unusual time signatures and martial rhythms, Gerald Fried and Robert Drasnin opted for a lighter approach in the second, employing harpsichords and bongos and by the third season, the music, like the show, had become more camp, exemplified by an R&B organ and saxophone version of the theme. The fourth season's attempt at seriousness was duly echoed by Richard Shores' somber scores.

Soundtrack albums

Although album recordings of the series had been made by Hugo Montenegro (ironically, Montenegro never worked on the series itself but did score an episode of Mission: Impossible), and many orchestras did cover versions of the title theme, it wouldn't be until 2002 that the first of three double-disc albums of original music from the series would be released through Film Score Monthly.

The Man From U.N.C.L.E.

Disc 1:

1. First Season Main Title (:45) – Jerry Goldsmith
2. The Vulcan Affair (14:01) – Jerry Goldsmith
3. The Deadly Games Affair (11:48) – Jerry Goldsmith
4. The Double Affair (6:51) – Morton Stevens
5. The Project Strigas Affair (7:14) – Walter Scharf
6. The King of Knaves Affair (12:22) – Jerry Goldsmith
7. The Fiddlesticks Affair (6:30) – Lalo Schifrin
8. Meet Mr.Solo (2:05) – Jerry Goldsmith
9. First Season End Title (:49) – Jerry Goldsmith
10. Second Season End Title (:49) – Jerry Goldsmith, arranged by Lalo Schifrin
11. Alexander the Greater Affair (13:12) – Gerald Fried

Disc 2:

1. The Foxes and Hounds Affair (5:16) – Robert Drasnin

2. The Discotheque Affair (8:49) – Gerald Fried
3. The Re-Collectors Affair (6:29) – Robert Drasnin
4. The Arabian Affair (5:29) – Gerald Fried
5. The Tigers Are Coming Affair (4:20) – Robert Drasnin
6. The Cherry Blossom Affair (5:12) – Gerald Fried
7. The Dippy Blonde Affair (7:50) – Robert Drasnin
8. Third Season End Title (:39) – Jerry Goldsmith, arr. Gerald Fried
9. The Her Master's Voice Affair (4:50) – Gerald Fried
10. The Monks of St.Thomas Affair (7:37) – Gerald Fried
11. The Pop Art Affair (4:50) – Robert Drasnin
12. Fourth Season Main Title (:32) – Jerry Goldsmith, arr. unknown
13. The Summit-Five Affair (5:52) – Richard Shores
14. The "J" for Judas Affair (8:03) – Richard Shores

The Man From U.N.C.L.E. Volume 2

Disc 1:

1. First Season End Title (1:16) – Jerry Goldsmith
2. The Vulcan Affair suite No.2 (9:59) – Jerry Goldsmith
3. The Iowa Scuba Affair (6:54) – Morton Stevens
4. The Shark Affair (7:55) – Walter Scharf
5. The Deadly Games Affair suite No.2 (3:40) – Jerry Goldsmith
6. Meet Mr. Solo (1:45) – Jerry Goldsmith
7. The Giuoco Piano Affair (3:23) – Walter Scharf
8. The King of Knaves Affair suite No.2 (3:40) – Jerry Goldsmith
9. First Season Main Title (revised) (:56) – Jerry Goldsmith, arr. Morton Stevens
10. The Deadly Decoy Affair (4:32) – Walter Scharf
11. The Spy With My Face (5:12) – Morton Stevens
12. Second Season Main Title (:37) – Jerry Goldsmith, arr. Lalo Schifrin
13. Alexander the Greater Affair (1:25) – Gerald Fried
14. The Ultimate Computer Affair (5:00) – Lalo Schifrin
15. The Very Important Zombie Affair (4:10) – Gerald Fried
16. The Dippy Blonde Affair (2:01) – Robert Drasnin
17. The Deadly Goddess Affair (2:31) – Gerald Fried
18. The Moonglow Affair (7:09) – Gerald Fried

Disc 2:

1. One of Our Spies is Missing (3:08) – Jerry Goldsmith, arr. Gerald Fried
2. Third Season Main Title (:31) – Jerry Goldsmith, arr. Gerald Fried
3. The Sort of Do-It-Yourself Dreadful Affair (6:39) – Gerald Fried

4. The Galatea Affair (5:36) – Robert Drasnin
5. The Pop Art Affair (4:34) – Robert Drasnin
6. The Come With Me to the Casbah Affair (4:16) – Gerald Fried
7. The Off-Broadway Affair (7;12) – Gerald Fried
8. The Concrete Overcoat Affair (6:48) – Nelson Riddle
9. The Napoleon's Tomb Affair (5:17) – Gerald Fried
10. Fourth Season Main Title (alternate) (:37) – Jerry Goldsmith, arr. Gerald Fried
11. Fourth Season End Title (:36) – Jerry Goldsmith, arr. Robert Armbruster?
12. The Test Tube Killer Affair (7:05) – Gerald Fried
13. The Prince of Darkness Affair (11:39) – Richard Shores
14. The Seven Wonders of the World Affair (11:46) – Richard Shores

The Man From U.N.C.L.E. Volume 3: Featuring The Girl From U.N.C.L.E.

Disc 1:

1. First Season Main Title (revised/extended) (1:00) – Jerry Goldsmith, arr. Morton Stevens
2. Jerry Goldsmith Medley (2:57)
3. The Quadripartite Affair (3:27) – Walter Scharf
4. The Double Affair, suite no. 2 (6:20) – Morton Stevens
5. Belly Laughs (2:21) – Jerry Goldsmith
6. The Finny Foot Affair (4:51) – Morton Stevens
7. The Fiddlesticks Affair, suite no. 2 (5:17) – Lalo Schifrin
8. The Yellow Scarf Affair (3:35) – Morton Stevens
9. Meet Mr. Solo (3:03) – Jerry Goldsmith
10. The Spy with my Face (4:09) – Morton Stevens
11. The Discotheque Affair, suite no. 2 (4:31) – Gerald Fried
12. The Nowhere Affair (2:48) – Robert Drasnin
13. U.N.C.L.E. A Go Go (3:05) – Gerald Fried
14. The Bat Cave Affair (4:42) – Gerald Fried
15. One of Our Spies is Missing (1:09) – Gerald Fried
16. The Monks of St. Thomas Affair, suite no. 2 (3:46) – Gerald Fried
17. The Spy in the Green Hat (3:19) – Jerry Goldsmith, arr. Gerald Fried and Robert Armbruster
18. Gerald Fried Medley (7:21)
19. The Karate Killers (1:51) – Gerald Fried
20. Richard Shores Medley (6:37)

Disc 2:

1. The Girl From U.N.C.L.E. Main Title (:34) – Jerry Goldsmith, arr. Dave Grusin
2. The Dog-gone Affair (5:28) – Dave Grusin
3. The Prisoner of Zalamar Affair (6:32) – Richard Shores

4. The Mother Muffin Affair (10:59) – Dave Grusin
5. The Mata Hari Affair (7:44) – Dave Grusin
6. The Montori Device Affair (5:31) – Richard Shores
7. The Horns-of-the-Dilemma Affair (2:05) – Jack Marshall
8. The Girl From U.N.C.L.E. End Title (:39) – Jerry Goldsmith, arr. Dave Grusin
9. The Deadly Quest Affair: Teaser (3:57)
10. The Deadly Quest Affair: Act I (7:48)
11. The Deadly Quest Affair: Act II (9:07)
12. The Deadly Quest Affair: Act III (7:24)
13. The Deadly Quest Affair: Act IV (8:06)

Tracks 9–13 Jerry Goldsmith, ad. and arr. Robert Armbruster:

FSM also released **The Spy With My Face: Music From *The Man From U.N.C.L.E.* Movies**, a disc of music specifically written for the feature film versions culled from episodes of the series (**One Of Our Spies Is Missing** and **The Karate Killers** are particularly strongly represented, due to the original TV episodes – "The Bridge Of Lions Affair" and "The Five Daughters Affair" respectively – having been tracked with music written for other episodes).

To Trap A Spy (Jerry Goldsmith):

1. Main Title/Solo Strikes Again (Main Title) (1:19)
2. The Kiss Off/Main Title (Meet Mr. Solo/End Title) (1:54)

The Spy With My Face (Morton Stevens):

3. Main Title (4:09)
4. Phase Two/Sub Male/Bugged Bobo (3:09)
5. New Alps/Impostor's First Test/Cyanide Cigarette (2:52)
6. Incarcerated Swinging (5:01)
7. The Real McCoy/End Title (2:17)

One Spy Too Many (Gerald Fried):

8. Dog Fight on Wheels (Main Title) – Goldsmith, arr. Fried (2:56)
9. Briefcase/Follow That Spy (:55)
10. The Three Alexanders/The Great Design (2:45)
11. Farm/Skip Loader/Wrong Driver (2:28)
12. End Title – Goldsmith, arr. Schifrin (:31)

One Of Our Spies Is Missing (Gerald Fried):

13. Main Title – Goldsmith, arr. Fried (3:08)
14. Go-Go in Soho/Cat Jam (1:46)

15. Duel by Flashlight/Fat Vat/Bridge of Lions (3:36)

16. Love With the Proper Mannequin/Thrush Cycle (1:29)

17. Thrush Guards/The Sacrifice/Jordin's Demise (2:31)

18. Hot Tie (1:58)

19. End Title – Goldsmith, arr. Fried (:37)

The Spy In The Green Hat (Nelson Riddle):

20. Main Title – Goldsmith, arr. Fried/Robert Armbruster (2:09)

21. Sicilian Style/Sacre! (1:22)

22. Stilletto Tango/Wrong Uncle (1:52)

23. Von Kronen/Kit Kat Klub (1:29)

24. Mr. Impeccable/I Sure Do/Right! (1:38)

25. End Title – Goldsmith, arr. Fried/Armbruster (:32)

The Karate Killers (Gerald Fried):

26. Main Title – Goldsmith, arr. Fried/Search Party (2:46)

27. Coliseum a Go Go/Arrivederci/Drain Pipe (3:08)

28. Along the Seine/Anyone for Venice (2:45)

29. Snow Goons/Touchdown (02:30)

30. Sidewalks of Japan (1:40)

31. Karate & Stick Game (1:24)

32. Mod Wedding/End Cast (1:03)

The Helicopter Spies (Jerry Goldsmith, arr. Armbruster):

33. Main Title (2:01)

34. End Title (:25)

How To Steal The World (Richard Shores):

35. Crazy Airport (Main Title) (2:08)

36. Trouble in Hong Kong (End Title) (:37)

Guest stars and other actors

Apart from Solo, Kuryakin and Waverly, very few characters appeared on the show with any regularity. As a result, *The Man from U.N.C.L.E.* featured a large number of high-profile guest performers during its three and a half year run.

William Shatner and Leonard Nimoy appeared together in a 1964 episode, "The Project Strigas Affair", a full two years before *Star Trek* aired for the first time. Shatner played a heroic civilian recruited for an U.N.C.L.E. mission, and Nimoy played the villain's henchman. The villain is played by Werner Klemperer. James Doohan appeared in multiple episodes, each time as a different character.

Barbara Feldon played an U.N.C.L.E. translator eager for field work in "The Never-Never Affair," one year before becoming one of the stars of the very different spy series Get Smart. Robert Culp played the villain in 1964's "The Shark Affair".

Woodrow Parfrey appeared five times as a guest performer, although he never received an opening-title credit. Usually cast as a scientist, he played the primary villain in only one episode, "The Cherry Blossom Affair." Another five-time guest star was Jill Ireland, who at the time was married to David McCallum. "The Five Daughters Affair" featured a cameo appearance by Joan Crawford. Janet Leigh and Jack Palance appeared in "The Concrete Overcoat Affair" and Sonny and Cher made an appearance in the third season episode "The Hot Number Affair". Notable guest stars and other actors included: Richard Anderson, Joan Blondell, Sonny Bono, Roger Carmel, Leo G. Carroll, Cher, Joan Collins, Joan Crawford, Robert Culp, Kim Darby, Ivan Dixon, James Doohan, Barbara Feldon, Anne Francis, Jill Ireland, Allen Jenkins, Richard Kiel, Werner Klemperer, Angela Lansbury, Janet Leigh, David McCallum, Leslie Nielsen, Leonard Nimoy, William Marshall (film and television actor), Carroll O'Connor, Jack Palance, Woodrow Parfrey, Eleanor Parker, Slim Pickens, Vincent Price, Dorothy Provine, Cesar Romero, Kurt Russell, William Shatner, Nancy Sinatra, Terry-Thomas, Robert Vaughn, Fritz Weaver.

Props

Solo and Kuryakin, trained in martial arts, also had a range of useful spy equipment, including handheld satellite communicators to keep in contact with UNCLE headquarters. A catchphrase often heard was "Open Channel D" when agents used their pocket radios (originally disguised as cigarette packs, later as a cigarette case, and in following seasons, as pens). One of the original pen communicators now resides in the museum of the Central Intelligence Agency. The museum is not accessible to the public. Replicas have been made over the years for other displays, and this is the second-most-identifiable prop from the series (closely following the U.N.C.L.E. Special pistol).

Weaponry

One prop, often referred to as "The Gun," drew so much attention that it actually spurred considerable fan mail, often so addressed. Internally designated the "U.N.C.L.E. Special", it featured a modular semi-automatic weapon, originally based on the Mauser Model 1934 Pocket Pistol, but was unreliable, jamming constantly, and considered so small that it was dwarfed by the carbine accessories. It was soon replaced by the larger and more reliable Walther P38 pistol. The basic pistol could still be converted into a longer-range carbine by attaching a long barrel, extendable shoulder stock, Bushnell telescopic sight, and extended magazine. In its carbine mode, the pistol could fire on full automatic. This capability brought authorities to the set early on to investigate reports that the studio was manufacturing machine guns illegally. They threatened to confiscate the prop guns. It took a tour of the prop room to convince them that these were 'dummy' pistols incapable of firing live ammunition.

The long magazine was actually a standard magazine with a dummy extension on it, but it inspired several manufacturers to begin making long magazines for various pistols. While many of these continue to be available 40 years later, long magazines were not available for the P-38 for some years. However, they are now being custom made, as are reproduction parts for the U.N.C.L.E. carbine, and sold at "TheUncleGun.com". "Pictures" of their U.N.C.L.E. gun reproductions can also be seen on the official "Man From U.N.C.L.E. DVD set". The "U.N.C.L.E. Special"-configured Walther P38 would later become the distinctive alternate mode for the *Transformers* character Megatron, the evil leader of the Decepticons.

The P-38 fired the standard 9 mm bullet, although sometimes it was loaded with a special dart tipped with a fast-acting tranquilizer when it was preferable to have a live prisoner. The drug lasted, according to Solo, about two hours. THRUSH never bothered. As Solo commented in the pilot, "...THRUSH kills people like people kill flies. A careless gesture. A flick of the wrist...".

THRUSH had a range of weaponry, much of it only in development before being destroyed by the heroes; a notable item was the infra-red sniperscope, enabling them to target gunfire in darkness. A major design defect of the sniperscope (in the TV series) was that its image tube's power supply emitted a distinctive whining sound when operating and (in reality) relied on a searchlight to illuminate the target. It also required a heavy battery and cable arrangement to power the scope. This weapon was built around a U.S. Army-surplus M1 carbine with a vertical foregrip and barrel compensator, and using real Army surplus infrared scopes. We see the fully-equipped carbines only once, in "The Iowa Scuba Affair". After that, a mock-up of the scope was used to make handling easier.

A few of the third-and fourth-season episodes featured an "U.N.C.L.E. car", which was a modified "Piranha Coupe", a Chevrolet Corvair-based plastic-bodied car built in limited numbers by custom car designer Gene Winfield.

German small arms were well-represented in the series. Not only were P-38s popular (both as basis for the U.N.C.L.E. Special and in standard configuration), but also the Luger P-08 pistol. In the pilot episode "The Vulcan Affair," Illya Kuryakin is carrying a standard Army .45 pistol. The

"Broomhandle" Mauser carbines and MP40 machine pistols were favored by opponents, both THRUSH and non-THRUSH. U.N.C.L.E. also used the MP-40. Beginning in the third season, both U.N.C.L.E and THRUSH used rifles which were either the Spanish CETME or the Heckler & Koch G3, which was based on the CETME.

There were also an assortment of other weapons, ranging from sniper and military rifles to pistols of various caliber, plus swords, knives, bludgeons, staffs, chains, etc.

Awards and nominations

Emmy Awards

- 1965: Outstanding Individual Achievements in Entertainment – Actors and Performers (Nominated) – David McCallum
- 1965: Outstanding Program Achievements in Entertainment (Nominated) – Sam Rolfe
- 1966: Outstanding Continued Performance by an Actor in a Leading Role in a Dramatic Series (Nominated) – David McCallum
- 1966: Outstanding Dramatic Series (Nominated) – Norman Felton
- 1966: Outstanding Performance by an Actor in a Supporting Role in a Drama (Nominated) – Leo G. Carroll
- 1966: Individual Achievements in Music – Composition (Nominated) – Jerry Goldsmith
- 1967: Outstanding Performance by an Actor in a Supporting Role in a Drama (Nominated) – Leo G. Carroll

Golden Globes Awards

- 1965: Best TV Star – Male (Nominated) – Robert Vaughn
- 1966: Best TV Star – Male (Nominated) – Robert Vaughn
- 1966: Best TV Star – Male (Nominated) – David McCallum
- 1966: Best TV Show (Won)
- 1967: Best TV Show (Nominated)

Grammy Awards

- 1966: Best Original Score Written for a Motion Picture or Television Show (Nominated)- Lalo Schifrin, Morton Stevens, Walter Scharf, Jerry Goldsmith

Logie Awards

- 1966: Best Overseas Show (Won)

Spin-offs

The series was popular enough to generate a spin-off series, *The Girl from U.N.C.L.E.* The "girl" was first introduced during "The Moonglow Affair" (February 25, 1966) an episode of *The Man From U.N.C.L.E.* and was then played by Mary Ann Mobley. *The Girl from U.N.C.L.E.* spin-off series ran for one season, starring Stefanie Powers as agent "April Dancer" (a character name credited to Ian Fleming). There was some crossover between the two shows, and Leo G. Carroll played Mr. Waverly in both programs, becoming the second actor in American television to star as the same character in two separate series. (The first being Frank Cady who played General Store owner Sam Drucker on *Petticoat Junction, Green Acres* and *The Beverly Hillbillies*).

The Man From U.N.C.L.E. rated so highly in America and the UK that MGM and the producers decided to film extra footage (often more adult to evoke Bond films) for two of the first season episodes and release them to theaters after they had aired on TV. The episodes with the extra footage that made it to theaters were the original pilot, "The Vulcan Affair," retitled *To Trap a Spy*, and also from the first season, "The Double Affair" retitled as *The Spy with My Face*. Both had added sex and violence, new sub-plots and guest stars not in the original TV episodes. They were often released as an *U.N.C.L.E.* double-feature program first run in neighborhood theaters, bypassing the customary downtown movie palaces which were still thriving in the mid-'60s and where new movies usually played for weeks and even months before coming to outlying screens.

A selling point to seeing these films on the big screen back then was that they were being shown in color, at a time when most people had only black and white TVs (and indeed the two first-season episodes that were expanded to feature length, while filmed in color, were only broadcast in black and white). The words IN COLOR featured prominently on the trailers, TV spots, and posters for the film releases.

Subsequent two-part episodes, beginning with the second season premiere, "Alexander The Greater Affair," retitled *One Spy Too Many* for its theatrical release, were developed into one complete feature film with only occasional extra sexy and violent footage added to them, sometimes as just inserts. In the case of *One Spy Too Many*, a subplot featuring Yvonne Craig as an UNCLE operative carrying on a flirtatious relationship with Solo was also added the film (Craig does not appear in the television episodes).

All of the films were successful in many parts of the world, even those where the TV show did not air, sometimes surpassing box office receipts of the most recent Bond film. The later films were not released in America, only overseas, but the first few did well in American theaters and remain one of the rare examples of a television show released in paid theatrical engagements.

Among the films in this series:

- *To Trap a Spy* (1964)
- *The Spy with My Face* (1965)

- *One Spy Too Many* (1966)
- *One of Our Spies is Missing* (1966)
- *The Spy in the Green Hat* (1966)
- *The Karate Killers* (1967)
- *The Helicopter Spies* (1968)
- *How to Steal the World* (1968)

The U.N.C.L.E. fad also inspired a related series of books, some written by David McDaniel.

Spin-offs included a *Man from U.N.C.L.E.* digest-sized story magazine, board games, action-figures, and toy pistols.

Several comic strips based on the series were published. In the US, there was a Gold Key Comics comic book series (one based on the show), which ran for about a dozen issues. Entertainment Publishing released an eleven issue series of one- and two-part stories from January 1987 to September 1988 that updated U.N.C.L.E. to the Eighties, while largely ignoring the reunion TV-movie. A two-part comics story, "The Birds of Prey Affair" was put out by Millennium Publications in 1993, which showcased the return of a smaller, much more streamlined version of Thrush, controlled by Dr. Egret, who had melded with the Ultimate Computer. The script was written by Mark Ellis and Terry Collins with artwork by Nick Choles, and transplanted the characters into the present day.

Two *Man from U.N.C.L.E.* strips were originated for the British market in the 1960s (some Gold Key material was also reprinted), the most notable for *Lady Penelope* comic, which launched in January 1966. This was replaced by a *Girl from U.N.C.L.E.* strip in January 1967. *Man from U.N.C.L.E.* also featured in the short-lived title *Solo* (published between February and September 1967) and some text stories appeared in *TV Tornado*.

Reunion TV movie

A reunion telefilm, *The Return of the Man from U.N.C.L.E.*, subtitled *The Fifteen Years Later Affair* was broadcast on CBS in America on April 5, 1983, with Vaughn and McCallum reprising their roles, and Patrick Macnee replacing Leo G. Carroll as the head of U.N.C.L.E. A framed picture of Carroll appeared on his desk. The movie included a tribute to Ian Fleming via a cameo appearance by an unidentified secret agent with the initials "J.B." The part was played by one-time James Bond George Lazenby who was shown driving Bond's trademark vehicle, an Aston Martin DB5. One character, identifying him, says that it is "just like *On Her Majesty's Secret Service*," which was Lazenby's only Bond film.

The movie, written by Michael Sloan and directed by Ray Austin, briefly filled in the missing years. THRUSH has been put out of business, and the remaining leader was in prison. (His escape begins the story.) Illya has quit U.N.C.L.E. after a mission went sour and an innocent woman was killed, and now designs women's clothing at Vanya's in New York. Napoleon has been pushed out of U.N.C.L.E. and now sells computers, though he still carries his U.N.C.L.E. pen radio for sentimental reasons (which is how the organization is able to contact him after so many years).

Solo and Kuryakin are recalled to recapture the escapee and defeat **THRUSH** once and for all, but the movie misfired on a key point: instead of reuniting the agents on the mission—and showcasing their witty interaction—the agents were separated and paired with younger agents. Like most similar reunion films, this production was considered a trial balloon for a possible new series.

Although some personnel from the original series were involved (like composer Gerald Fried and director of photography Fred Koenekamp), the movie was not produced by Metro-Goldwyn-Mayer but by Michael Sloan Productions in association with Viacom Productions - Sloan, Vaughn and McCallum are pictured in the Michael Sloan Productions logo at the end of the movie.

Novels

Two dozen novels were based upon *Man from U.N.C.L.E.* and published between 1965 and 1968 (for a time, the most of any American-produced television series except for *Star Trek*, though there have now been more original novels published based upon *Alias* and *Buffy the Vampire Slayer*). Freed from the limitations of network television, these novels were generally grittier and more violent than the televised episodes. The series sold in the millions, and was the largest TV-novel tie-in franchise until surpassed by Star Trek novels.

1. *The Man from U.N.C.L.E.* (a.k.a. *The Thousand Coffins Affair*) – Michael Avallone
2. *The Doomsday Affair* – Harry Whittington
3. *The Copenhagen Affair* – John Oram
4. *The Dagger Affair* – David McDaniel
5. *The Mad Scientist Affair* – John T. Phillifent
6. *The Vampire Affair* – McDaniel
7. *The Radioactive Camel Affair* – Peter Leslie
8. *The Monster Wheel Affair* – McDaniel
9. *The Diving Dames Affair* – Leslie
10. *The Assassination Affair* – J. Hunter Holly
11. *The Invisibility Affair* – Buck Coulson and Gene DeWeese (writing as "Thomas Stratton")
12. *The Mind Twisters Affair* – "Stratton"
13. *The Rainbow Affair* – McDaniel
14. *The Cross of Gold Affair* – Ron Ellik and Fredric Langley (writing as "Fredric Davies")
15. *The Utopia Affair* – McDaniel
16. *The Splintered Sunglasses Affair* – Leslie
17. *The Hollow Crown Affair* – McDaniel
18. *The Unfair Fare Affair* – Leslie
19. *The Power Cube Affair* – Phillifent
20. *The Corfu Affair* – Phillifent

21. *The Thinking Machine Affair* – Joel Bernard
22. *The Stone Cold Dead in the Market Affair* – Oram
23. *The Finger in the Sky Affair* – Leslie.

Another volume, *The Final Affair*, also by David McDaniel, was completed but not published.[citation needed] Copies of the manuscript have circulated among fans for decades.[citation needed] Written *after* the series was cancelled, it was intended to provide a definitive conclusion to Solo and Ilya's adventures. At one time there were plans to publish *The Final Affair* in a limited deluxe edition, but the project failed.[citation needed] Another book, *The Catacombs and Dogma Affair*, has been mentioned in some sources, but it isn't listed as one of the official U.N.C.L.E. novels (it's possible it might be one of the above volumes, retitled, or it may be the unpublished second U.N.C.L.E.novel by J. Hunter Holly, which has been circulated in mimeographed form among fans).[citation needed] Volumes 10–15 and 17 of the series were only published in the United States.

Two science-fiction novels – *Genius Unlimited* by John Rackham (a pseudonym used by Phillifent) and *The Arsenal Out of Time* by McDaniel – appear to be rewrites of "orphaned" U.N.C.L.E novel outlines or manuscripts.

The Rainbow Affair is notable for its thinly-disguised cameo appearances by The Saint, Miss Marple, John Steed, Emma Peel, Tommy Hambledon (at whose flat Solo and Ilya encounter Steed and Peel), Neddie Seagoon, Father Brown, a retired, elderly Sherlock Holmes, and Dr. Fu Manchu. The novel uses the same chapter title format that Leslie Charteris used in his *Saint* novels. (The title of one of the theatrical versions of UNCLE episodes, *The Spy in the Green Hat*, is very close to the title of *The Man in the Green Hat*, one of the "Hambledon" novels by "Manning Coles".)

Whitman Books also published three hardcover novels aimed at young readers and based upon the series. The first two books break the naming convention "The .... Affair" used by all other U.N.C.L.E. fiction and episodes:

1. *The Affair of the Gunrunners' Gold* – Brandon Keith
2. *The Affair of the Gentle Saboteur* – Brandon Keith
3. *The Calcutta Affair* – George S. Elrick

A children's storybook written by Walter Gibson entitled *The Coin of El Diablo Affair* was also published.

The aforementioned digest magazine based upon *Man from U.N.C.L.E.* and often featured original novellas that were not published anywhere else. These novellas, published under the house name "Robert Hart Davis," were actually written by such authors as John Jakes, Dennis Lynds, and Bill Pronzini. There were 24 issues running monthly from February 1966 till January 1968, inclusive.

Science fiction writer Jack Jardine (writing as Larry Maddock) originally came up with an idea for a "Man From U.N.C.L.E." novel called "The Flying Saucer Affair", but it was A) deemed too sci-fi for the series' concept, and B) written shortly before the series' cancellation. He later adapted this novel into his "Agent of T.E.R.R.A." series, which enjoyed a brief run of four titles altogether, and were published by ACE Books. They are:

"Agent Of T.E.R.R.A. #1: The Flying Saucer Gambit", "Agent Of T.E.R.R.A. #2: The Golden Goddess Gambit", "Agent Of T.E.R.R.A. #3: The Emerald Elephant Gambit", and "Agent Of T.E.R.R.A. #4: The Time Trap Gambit" (the latter title dispensed with the "Agent of T.E.R.R.A." moniker).

DVD releases

In November 2007, after coming to an agreement with Warner Home Video, Time-Life released a 41 DVD set (region 1) for direct order, with sales through stores scheduled for fall 2008. An earlier release by Anchor Bay, allegedly set for 2006, was apparently scuttled because of a dispute over the rights to the series with Warner Brothers.

A region 2 DVD (PAL for Europe) release of *The Man from U.N.C.L.E.* movies was released on September 8, 2003. The DVD contains five of the eight movies, missing the following: *To Trap a Spy* (1964), *The Spy in the Green Hat* (1966) and *One of Our Spies is Missing* (1966).

On Oct. 21, 2008, the Time-Life set was released to retail outlets in Region 1 (North America) in a special all-seasons box set contained within a small briefcase. The complete-series set consists of 41 DVDs, including two discs of special features included exclusively with the box set. Included in the set was the *Solo* pilot episode, as well as one of the films, *One Spy Too Many*; to date this is the only Region 1 DVD release of the feature films.

Paramount Pictures and CBS Home Entertainment released *The Return of the Man from U.N.C.L.E.* to DVD in Region 1 on March 3, 2009.

U.N.C.L.E. in popular culture

During the show's original run, *The Man from U.N.C.L.E.* was parodied in an episode of *The Dick Van Dyke Show*, fittingly titled "The Man from My Uncle." In this episode, Rob Petrie (Van Dyke) allows his suburban house to be used as a stakeout for an unnamed government agency. They want to spy on one of his neighbors who has a deported nephew that may be back in the country illegally. Comedian Godfrey Cambridge guest stars as an agent whose name is Mr. Bond, a recurring joke in the episode. In the show's final scene, referred to in sitcom circles as the "tag," Rob is playing with the agent's walkie talkie and fantasizes that he is negotiating a hostage exchange with THRUSH. The show was also parodied by MGM itself on "The Mouse from H.U.N.G.E.R.", an episode of *Tom and Jerry*. The British TV series *The Avengers* featured an episode titled "The Girl from AUNTIE" (a double in-joke in the UK, where "Auntie" was a nickname for the BBC).

Robert Vaughn makes an uncredited cameo appearance as Napoleon Solo in a dinner party scene in the Doris Day film, *The Glass Bottom Boat*. Solo is shown at the bar (complete with U.N.C.L.E. theme music), operating his pen radio and giving Paul Lynde (as Homer Cripps) a smiling, almost lecherous look as he walks by in drag. Day's film plot is about an Earth-based secret zero-gravity test laboratory built to train astronauts.

Both Vaughn and David McCallum made brief appearances in character in a *Please Don't Eat the Daisies* TV episode titled "Cry UNCLE". The star of the show Patricia Crowley had costarred in the original UNCLE pilot *The Vulcan Affair*. The end credits of the episode, like *The Man from U.N.C.L.E.*, thanked the United Network Command for its co-operation. McCallum also hosted an episode of the popular 1960's TV variety show *Hullabaloo* as Illya Kuryakin.

Leo G. Carroll had a cameo on the first episode of Laugh In broadcast on Jan. 22, 1968 in which he spoofed U.N.C.L.E. Ironically that was the show that took over Uncle's timeslot when it was cancelled. A bartender at one of Laugh In's standing comedy sketch locations, a go-go party scene, he suddenly turns as he pulls out an U.N.C.L.E. pen radio and intones into it, "Open Channel D: Come in, Mr. Solo, I think I've found THRUSH headquarters!"

A British secret agent who always survived through ingenuity despite being ineffectual-looking and short-sighted appeared as 'The Man From B.U.N.G.L.E.' in the 1964 UK comic Wham!.

A season five episode of the 1980s adventure series *The A-Team* was entitled "The Say U.N.C.L.E. Affair" and featured both Vaughn and McCallum. Vaughn had a recurring role as a member of *The A-Team*'s cast at this point, playing General Stockwell, while McCallum appeared as Stockwell's former espionage partner, Ivan. The episode was loaded with in-jokes referencing the 1960s series. The signature bongo drums & pan from *The Man From U.N.C.L.E.* was used whenever scenes changed in that episode. McCallum played one of the few characters ever to have been killed in an *A-Team* episode.

In an episode of *Tales from the Darkside* titled "The Impressionist", a government organization named U.N.C.L.E. hires an impersonator to talk with an alien.

A few brief references to U.N.C.L.E. are made in *The League of Extraordinary Gentlemen: Black Dossier*, along with appearances by characters from *The Avengers*, *Danger Man*, and *The Prisoner*. U.N.C.L.E. is never called by name in the story, although Waverly is mentioned, albeit by his last name only, as a schoolmate of Billy Bunter's at Greyfriars and also a member of a Cambridge Five.

In his 1980 album *Get Happy!!*, Elvis Costello wrote the track "Man Called Uncle". Although the lyrics do not make any references to the show, the song has a Sixties upbeat feel connected with the original "Man from U.N.C.L.E" soundtrack. An Argentinian Funk duo was named Illya Kuryaki and the Valderramas honoring the fictitious spy. Alma Cogan paid a similar tribute to the Russian agent in her single "Love Ya Illya", released in 1966 under the pseudonym "Angela and the Fans". In the 1980s Cleaners From Venus penned "Ilya Kuryakin Looked at Me"; the song was later covered by The Jennifers. The English 2 Tone band The Specials made an instrumental song called "Napoleon Solo." It was also the name of a Danish 2 Tone band. Space–surf band Man or Astro-man? covered the theme song for their 1994 EP *Astro Launch*. The Pet Shop Boys song "Building A Wall", from their 2009 album 'Yes', contains the lyric "Jesus and the Man From U.N.C.L.E".

In the video game *Duke Nukem 3D*, there is a secret military base, and hidden on a telephone booth it says "U.N.C.L.E." rather than the typical "PHONE." Using this phone leads to a hidden area.

In the Randall Garrett novel *Too Many Magicians*, character Tia Einzig's father's brother Neapeler is said to come from the Isle of Mann, and thus is the Uncle from Mann. "Neapeler Einzig" is recognizably a variant of "Napoleon Solo" ("Neapel" is the German name for Naples; "einzig" is German for "only" or "unique"). And Tia's Uncle has a friend, "Colin MacDavid", whose name is recognizably a variant of the actor's name "David McCallum".

The British comedian Ben Elton starred in two series of his own stand-up comedy and sketch show entitled *The Man from Auntie*, in 1990 and 1994. The title of the show was a play on the title of *The Man from UNCLE* and the fact that 'Auntie' is a nickname for the BBC.

Forty years after the debut of this series, its stars appeared on TV, Vaughn in the British caper series *Hustle* and McCallum in the American military crime investigation series *NCIS*. In the season two *NCIS* episode "The Meat Puzzle," Leroy Gibbs mentions that when he was younger, Ducky Mallard looked like Illya Kuryakin. To which 30-something Kate asks, "Who?"

In an interview for a retrospective television special, David McCallum told of a visit to the White House during which, while he was being escorted to meet the President, a Secret Service agent told him "You're the reason I got this job." [1]

On the popular morning drive time radio show Bob and Brian morning show, out of Milwaukee WI, Brian has made himself the Man from U.N.C.L.E regarding sports. In his case he "rules" on all sports Uniforms Nicknames Colors Logos and Emblems and deems them appropriate or not.

In the video game *Team Fortress 2*, one of the achievements for the Spy, The Man from P.U.N.C.T.U.R.E, is a reference to the show.

In a fourth-season episode of *Mad Men*, "The Chrysanthemum and the Sword," Sally Draper masturbates while watching a scene involving Illya Kuryakin on *The Man from U.N.C.L.E.* episode "The Hong Kong Shilling Affair" (broadcast on March 15, 1965) at a sleepover.

In the HBO movie Temple Grandin, the title character is a big fan of the show, and she refers to it several times. In the opening sequence, Temple describes for her Aunt a scene in the show where a man with a shotgun says to Illya Kuryakin, "Would you like for me to open the gate?" Temple finds the line to be hilarious. Later, while she is in college, she joins other students in her dorm in the common room to watch the show. Short clips from the show are shown.

See also
- Napoleon Solo
- Illya Kuryakin

External links
- *The Man from U.N.C.L.E.* [2] at the Internet Movie Database
- *The Man from U.N.C.L.E.* [3] at TV.com
- Encyclopedia of Television [4]
- CIA Spy Fi Archives [5] including U.N.C.L.E. artifacts
- The Television Tie-In Affair [6] – images of comics, magazines and memorabilia
- Site devoted to Napoleon Solo [7]
- Spywise: "The U.N.C.L.E. Movie That Never Was" [8]
- "The Man from U.N.C.L.E.: A Retrospective" by Kathleen Crighton [9]
- Production history and DVD review of complete series [10]
- Time-Life's Nov. 2007 DVD collection [11]
- A blog detailing a fan's effort to build a functional U.N.C.L.E. Special [12]

Death

Victim impact statement

A **victim impact statement** is a written or oral statement made as part of the judicial legal process, which allows a victim of crime the opportunity to speak during the sentencing of their attacker or at subsequent parole hearings. In some instances videotaped statements are permitted.

History

Victim impact statements originate from the Manson Murders in 1969. One of those killed was actress Sharon Tate. A decade after the murders, Tate's mother, Doris, in response to the growing cult status of the killers and the possibility that any of them might be granted parole, organized a public campaign against what she considered shortcomings in the state's corrections system which led to amendments to the California criminal law in 1982, which allowed crime victims and their families to make victim impact statements during sentencing and at parole hearings. Doris Tate was the first person to make such an impact statement under the new law, when she spoke at the parole hearing of one of her daughter's killers, Charles "Tex" Watson. She later said that she believed the changes in the law had afforded her daughter dignity that had been denied her before, and that she had been able to "help transform Sharon's legacy from murder victim to a symbol of victims' rights".

Overview

One purpose of the statement is to allow the person or persons most directly affected by the crime to address the court during the decision making process. It is seen to personalize the crime and elevate the status of the victim. From the victim's point of view it is regarded as valuable in aiding their emotional recovery from their ordeal. It has also been suggested they may confront an offender with the results of their crime and thus aid rehabilitation.

Another purpose of the statement is to inform a court of the harm suffered by the victim if the court is required to, or has the option of, having regard to the harm suffered by the victim in deciding the sentence.

In cases of crimes resulting in death, the right to speak is extended to family members. In some jurisdictions there are very different rules on how victim impact statements from family members may be regarded. This is because it is seen as unprincipled that different punishments for death are given according to the how much the victim is missed, or conversely that someone's death is relatively less harmful if they have no family. In the circumstance of death, some jurisdictions have described victim impact statements from family members as 'irrelevant' to sentence but not 'unimportant' to the process: they are valued for restorative purposes but cannot differentiate punishment for causing death.

In general terms, the person making the statement is allowed to discuss specifically the direct harm or trauma they have suffered and problems that have resulted from the crime such as loss of income. Some jurisdictions allow for attaching medical and psychiatric reports that demonstrate harm to the victim. They can also discuss the impact the crime has had on their ambitions or plans for the future, and how this also impacted their extended family.

Some jurisdictions permit statements to express what they deem to be an appropriate punishment or sentence for the criminal.

Some jurisdictions expressly forbid any proposal or suggestion on punishment or sentencing. Among other reasons, this is because the sentencing process is solely the domain of the judge who consider many more factors than harm to victims. Allowing suggestions on punishment or sentence can create a false hope of the eventual sentence and undermine the notion of restorative justice.

United States

The first such statement in the United States was presented in 1976 in Fresno, California although it was not passed as law in California until 1982, possibly because of Theresa Saldana's near-fatal attack that year.

In 1982, the Final Report of the President's Task Force on Victims of Crime recommended that "judges allow for, and give appropriate weight to, input at sentencing from victims of violent crime." In 1992, the United States Attorney General released 24 recommendations to strengthen the criminal justice system's treatment of crime victims. The Attorney General endorsed the use of victim impact statements and stated that judges should "provide for hearing and considering the victims' perspective at sentencing and at any early release proceedings."

In 1991, the Supreme Court of the United States held that a victim impact statement in the form of testimony was allowed during the sentencing phase of a trial in *Payne v. Tennessee* 501 U.S. 808 [1] (1991). It ruled that the admission of such statements did not violate the Constitution and that the statements could be ruled as admissible in death penalty cases.

By 1997, 44 of the American states allowed the presentation of victim impact statements during its official process, although until 1991 these statements were held as inadmissible in cases where the death penalty was sought.

The law varies in different states, and while most states allow statements to be made during the sentencing phase of the trial, Indiana and Texas allow for statements to also be made after sentencing.

Australia

The State of South Australia enacted law in 1988 specifically providing for Victim Impact Statements in the sentencing process, and other States followed with legislation that either provides specifically or generally for the tendering of victim impact statements as part of the sentencing process.

Among current issues with victim impact statements is their relative newness and a lack of research into their actual effectiveness against their theoretical goals. There are occasionally legal issues surrounding the admissibility of facts in a victim impact statement that are materially adverse to an offender.

In the State of Queensland, the Director of Public Prosecution guidelines require prosecutors to remove inappropriate or inflammatory material from Victim Impact Statements prior to them being submitted before a court to prevent any such issues.

Finland

In Finland, the victim has a right to recommend a punishment different from the one recommended by the prosecution.

See also

- Victimology
- Victim Support
- *Spoilt Rotten: The Toxic Cult of Sentimentality*

External links

- Criminal Justice Intervention [2]
- *A Victim's Right to Speak, A Nation's Responsibility to Listen.* Article from Office for Victims of Crime, sponsored by the United States Department of Justice. [3]
- Darkness to Light - Victim Impact Statement. [4]
- Article relating to variations in the right of victims to present statement between various US States. [5]
- Lawlink. New South Wales, Australia, Advice and Information, Victims of Crime - Victim Impact Statement. [6]
- *Victim Impact Statement*, Sina A. Vogt (German) [7]

Article Sources and Contributors

Sharon Tate *Source*: http://en.wikipedia.org/?oldid=390055236 *Contributors*:

Roman Polanski *Source*: http://en.wikipedia.org/?oldid=389033927 *Contributors*:

Philippe Forquet *Source*: http://en.wikipedia.org/?oldid=346848477 *Contributors*: 1 anonymous edits

Doris Tate *Source*: http://en.wikipedia.org/?oldid=390561561 *Contributors*: Kumioko

Barabbas (1961 film) *Source*: http://en.wikipedia.org/?oldid=370172685 *Contributors*: DeWaine

Hemingway's Adventures of a Young Man *Source*: http://en.wikipedia.org/?oldid=382146751 *Contributors*: 1 anonymous edits

The Americanization of Emily *Source*: http://en.wikipedia.org/?oldid=373600558 *Contributors*: B3t

Eye of the Devil *Source*: http://en.wikipedia.org/?oldid=382007776 *Contributors*: Hydrargyrum

Don't Make Waves *Source*: http://en.wikipedia.org/?oldid=383431693 *Contributors*: Sreejithk2000

The Fearless Vampire Killers *Source*: http://en.wikipedia.org/?oldid=389208749 *Contributors*: Dutzi

Valley of the Dolls (film) *Source*: http://en.wikipedia.org/?oldid=383735979 *Contributors*: Tkreuz

Rosemary's Baby (film) *Source*: http://en.wikipedia.org/?oldid=390372557 *Contributors*: Pechblaende

The Wrecking Crew (1969 film) *Source*: http://en.wikipedia.org/?oldid=384320061 *Contributors*: Falcon8765

The Thirteen Chairs *Source*: http://en.wikipedia.org/?oldid=389784258 *Contributors*: Trivialist

Julie Andrews *Source*: http://en.wikipedia.org/?oldid=389589007 *Contributors*: 1 anonymous edits

Tony Curtis *Source*: http://en.wikipedia.org/?oldid=390526432 *Contributors*: Wikiwatcher1

Mister Ed *Source*: http://en.wikipedia.org/?oldid=389141036 *Contributors*: Retropolis1

The Beverly Hillbillies *Source*: http://en.wikipedia.org/?oldid=389248719 *Contributors*: 1 anonymous edits

The Man from U.N.C.L.E. *Source*: http://en.wikipedia.org/?oldid=390545140 *Contributors*: Art LaPella

Victim impact statement *Source*: http://en.wikipedia.org/?oldid=390210329 *Contributors*: Jprw

Image Sources, Licenses and Contributors

File:Sharon Tate in Eye of the Devil trailer 3.jpg *Source*: http://en.wikipedia.org/w/index.php?title=File:Sharon_Tate_in_Eye_of_the_Devil_trailer_3.jpg *License*: unknown *Contributors*: Self made screen capture from a public domain film trailer Licencing information : http://www.creativeclearance.com/guidelines.html#D2

File:Max Baer Jr, Nancy Kulp and Sharon Tate in The Beverly Hillbillies, The Giant Jackrabbit episode.jpg *Source*: http://en.wikipedia.org/w/index.php?title=File:Max_Baer_Jr,_Nancy_Kulp_and_Sharon_Tate_in_The_Beverly_Hillbillies,_The_Giant_Jackrabbit_episode.jpg *License*: unknown *Contributors*: Television screenshot Licencing information : http://pdmdb.org/content.asp?contentid=806

File:Roman Polanski gwiazda Lodz.jpg *Source*: http://en.wikipedia.org/w/index.php?title=File:Roman_Polanski_gwiazda_Lodz.jpg *License*: Creative Commons Attribution-Sharealike 2.5 *Contributors*: User:HuBar

File:Roman Polanski Emmanuelle Seigner Cannes.jpg *Source*: http://en.wikipedia.org/w/index.php?title=File:Roman_Polanski_Emmanuelle_Seigner_Cannes.jpg *License*: Creative Commons Attribution-Sharealike 3.0 *Contributors*: Georges Biard

File:Roman Polanski..jpg *Source*: http://en.wikipedia.org/w/index.php?title=File:Roman_Polanski..jpg *License*: Creative Commons Attribution-Sharealike 2.5 *Contributors*: User:Nikita

File:Flag of Italy.svg *Source*: http://en.wikipedia.org/w/index.php?title=File:Flag_of_Italy.svg *License*: Public Domain *Contributors*: see below

File:Eye of the Devil trailer title .jpg *Source*: http://en.wikipedia.org/w/index.php?title=File:Eye_of_the_Devil_trailer_title_.jpg *License*: unknown *Contributors*: Self made screen capture from a public domain film trailer Licencing information : http://www.creativeclearance.com/guidelines.html#D2

Image:Flag of the United Kingdom.svg *Source*: http://en.wikipedia.org/w/index.php?title=File:Flag_of_the_United_Kingdom.svg *License*: Public Domain *Contributors*: User:Zscout370

Image:Flag of the United States.svg *Source*: http://en.wikipedia.org/w/index.php?title=File:Flag_of_the_United_States.svg *License*: Public Domain *Contributors*: User:Dbenbenn, User:Indolences, User:Jacobolus, User:Technion, User:Zscout370

File:JulieAndrews face.jpg *Source*: http://en.wikipedia.org/w/index.php?title=File:JulieAndrews_face.jpg *License*: GNU Free Documentation License *Contributors*: Original uploader was BFlatOctava at en.wikipedia

File:2009-0314-LV-002-TonyCurtis.jpg *Source*: http://en.wikipedia.org/w/index.php?title=File:2009-0314-LV-002-TonyCurtis.jpg *License*: Creative Commons Attribution 2.5 *Contributors*: Bobak Ha'Eri

The cover image herein is used under a Creative Commons License and may be reused or reproduced under that same license.

CPSIA information can be obtained at www.ICGtesting.com
Printed in the USA
LVOW11s0011300913

354656LV00006B/78/P